KU-462-039

THE MAN GOD MASTERED

'GOD MUST WIN'

From Calvin's letter to the faithful in France, 1559

The portrait of Calvin reproduced on the jacket is from a sixteenth-century painting discovered in Paris. It is taken from the book, *La Vie ardente du Premier Refuge français*, by F. Fournier-Marcigny, Editions du Mont-Blanc, Geneva.

A BRIEF BIOGRAPHY OF JOHN CALVIN

The Man
God Mastered

by
JEAN CADIER

Translated from the French by O. R. Johnston

LONDON
INTER-VARSITY FELLOWSHIP
39 Bedford Square, W. C. 1

© Editions Labor et Fides, Geneva

English translation © Inter-Varsity Fellowship

Translated from *Calvin: L'homme que
Dieu a dompté* by permission of
Editions Labor et Fides

First Edition in English . . . November, 1960

Reprinted . . . December, 1964

Made and printed in England by
STAPLES PRINTERS LIMITED
at their Rochester, Kent, establishment

TRANSLATOR'S NOTE

JEAN CADIER's book is a fine introduction to the life and work of Calvin, and not the least of its merits is that it is eminently readable. In this translation I have aimed primarily at rendering the French text in English as clear and pleasant as M. Cadier's French. However, a certain freedom with the language of the main narrative has been balanced by a more strictly literal rendering of the quotations.

On the principle that the average reader will have neither the time nor the facilities to refer to learned journals (e.g. the *Bulletin de la Société d'Histoire du Protestantisme française—B.H.P.F.* in references), a number of the footnotes of the French edition have been omitted, though references to major sources, together with other material of some intrinsic interest, have been retained.

The Bibliographical Notes at the end of the French edition consisted almost entirely of French works. For the new Bibliographical Note in this edition I am indebted to the Rev. Dr. J. I. Packer, whose survey takes into account the needs of the general English reader and the rapidly increasing number of works in this field. I should also like to thank M. Robert Delanoë for his help with a number of passages involving obsolete and technical expressions.

O. R. JOHNSTON

CONTENTS

ILLUSTRATIONS

The illustrations on pages 15, 20, 51, 63, 99, 108, 166 have
been taken from the well-known work of E. Doumergue: *Jean
Calvin, les Hommes et les Choses de son Temps*. Those on pages 79
and 147 are taken from the work of F. Fournier-Marcigny:
La Vie ardente du Premier Refuge français.

FOREWORD

THERE are few figures as well known as that of Calvin. The story of his life has often been told, and after the fine biographies by Emile Doumergue, Walker, J. D. Benoit, F. Wendel and recently by Albert-Marie Schmidt, we wondered whether it was really necessary to devote still more space to the Genevan Reformer.

However we yielded to the kindly insistence of the Editions Labor et Fides and we have penned this portrait of a victor. For this man, whose health was always so uncertain and who always looked so sickly, was one of the great warriors of the Spirit; though weak, he is a conqueror. Not indeed in his own strength, but in the might of the Lord who had truly conquered and overcome him. His victory was fashioned out of a continual self-denial, for he had taken as his motto, 'I offer to God my heart as a sacrifice.'

No original discoveries will be found in these pages, no controversies, no theological discussions, but simply certain historical data essential for the knowledge of a personality. There will also be found here, we hope, a testimony to the indomitable courage of the one whom God used to give to the French Reformation of the sixteenth century a leader, and to the Reformation movement of succeeding centuries its greatest theologian.

J. CADIER

CHAPTER I

IN THE SHADOW OF A CATHEDRAL

THE traveller on his way from Paris to Saint-Quentin will pass through a little city dominated by a great cathedral when he is still some thirty miles from his destination. This city is Noyon. The church rises above tightly-packed roofs, and gives the town its character. One guesses that for centuries ecclesiastical power has been exercised here in a massive and authoritarian manner. It was here, in the sixth century, that Saint Médard set up his episcopal seat. Here, in the following century, Saint Éloi, the famous counsellor of King Dagobert, founded an abbey. In the eighth century, Noyon became the most important religious centre of northern France. It was in this cathedral that kings were consecrated: Charlemagne in 768, Hugues Capet in 987. The Middle Ages, too, saw the building of numerous convents and churches in this district.

It was inevitable that a struggle should arise here against the heavy yoke of the Church. The commune movement at the beginning of the twelfth century led to the formation of one of those communes through which the bourgeois tried to struggle against the pretensions of the bishops. The resistance was short-lived, it seems; but it did not fail to leave its mark on the character of the city.

It was in this city with its clerical tradition and, as it were, in the shadow of the cathedral itself, that John

Calvin was born on July 10, 1509. His father, Gérard Cauvin,[1] had left the tiny village of Pont-l'Evêque, nearby, where his ancestors had been boatmen on the River Oise, to become the business manager of the clergy of Noyon. He was successively chapter attorney, secretary of the official principal, procurator fiscal of the county and the canons' proctor in matters ecclesiastical. In these various capacities he had charge of the church's wealth. It cannot be said that the best side of church life is seen from the study of the work of an ecclesiastical procurator. There are too many quarrels, too many money matters are dealt with, too many material ambitions bound up with religious questions come to light. It is not without interest to underline the fact that two French Reformers were sons of chapter clerks: Guillaume Farel and John Calvin. From their childhood, hearing the story of the difficulties with which their parents grappled in the temporal administration of the church's wealth, they had the vision of a different community, a spiritual one.

One day, however, the relations between Gérard Cauvin and the chapter of Noyon became so strained that open warfare broke out. When Calvin's father died in 1531, he was under ecclesiastical censure and it was only with great difficulty that his elder son Charles obtained permission for his father to be buried in consecrated ground. A short time afterwards, Charles himself was excommunicated, long before his brother, John, had taken a stand for the evangelical cause. Charles was to die in 1537 without having been reconciled with the Church and refusing the sacraments, as we shall see later. Calvin's family was always in some way or other too mixed up in

---

[1] The Reformer latinized his name Cauvin to Calvinus, hence the usual form Calvin.

the affairs of the church not to be in revolt against the dictatorial aspirations of the clergy.[1]

However, procurator Gérard Cauvin saw that his sons were provided with benefices. In 1518, Charles received a quarter of the revenue from the altar of la Gésine (*Virgini puerperae*) which stood at the entrance to the cathedral chancel. In 1521, at the age of twelve, John received another portion from this altar of la Gésine. This portion was made up of dues arising from estates, one of which was situated at Espeville. This is the origin of one of the names which Calvin assumed: he sometimes signed himself Charles d'Espeville. In 1527 another benefice was granted to him, that of the parish of Saint-Martin-de-Martheville, which he exchanged two years later for the parish of Pont-l'Evêque, the village of his ancestors. By means of these benefices, Gérard Cauvin wished to make it possible for his sons to pursue a scholastic career. They served at this time as a type of educational maintenance grant.

Thus endowed, the young man actually began his studies in a school at Noyon, called the Collège des Capettes on account of a little cape which the pupils wore. From that time onwards his fellow pupils were certain young noblemen of the district, and in particular those of the Hangest family, who had provided several bishops for the episcopal chair at Noyon. Two young men in this family, Joachim and Yves de Montmor, were John Calvin's companions, first at Noyon and later at Paris. One of their brothers was to join Calvin later at Geneva. Two of their cousins were to become great Huguenot leaders. The Reformer was thus, in his youth, on

[1] In his book *La Jeunesse de Calvin* (Paris, 1888), Abel Lefranc laid much stress on these facts. He saw in them one of the foremost causes of Calvin's conversion.

intimate terms with the young nobility in his native town.[1]

His family belonged to the upper middle class. Gérard Cauvin had been made a citizen of the town in 1497. He married Jeanne Le Franc, daughter of a former innkeeper who was also a citizen well known in the town. Her reputation was that of a pious woman of remarkable beauty. Calvin does not speak of his mother in his writings, and the allusions which he makes to his youth are rare. In the *Treatise on Relics* he says in passing, speaking of the fragments of the relics of St. Anne: 'Amongst others I remember that I kissed one part in the Abbey of Ourscamp, near Noyon.'[2] Perhaps he had as a child accompanied his mother on this pilgrimage and seen in some niche or other 'a quaint figure, squinting and grimacing'.[3]

Can we discover the house in which Calvin was born? As it lay on the traditional invasion route, the little city of Noyon was devastated many times. In 1552, at the time of the passage of the Imperial Armies, fire ravaged the town.[4] On this occasion Calvin wrote to Ambroise Blaurer, pastor at Bienne: 'I am living longer than my native land, which I should never have thought possible. The town in which I was born has been entirely destroyed by fire. Every day we are brought to learn of new disasters throughout Picardie. These disasters are of so little avail

[1] Out of gratitude he was to dedicate his first work of humanistic learning, the *De Clementia*, to the abbot of St. Eloi, Claude de Hangest.

[2] *Op. Calv.*, VI, p. 442. Cf. Doumergue: *Jean Calvin, les Hommes et les Choses de son Temps*, I, p. 41.

[3] Inst. I, xi. 13.

[4] 'Whilst the horses of the French army were drinking at the Rhine, two detachments of Imperial forces (part of the 60,000 men raised by Charles V against Henri II) were devastating Picardy and Champagne. At the head of one of these forces the Count de Reuth penetrated as far as Noyon. He had burned everything as he came, and he then burned this town....' Lacretelle, *Histoire de France pendant des Guerres de Religion* (Paris, 1844), I, p. 146.

I. Room of Jeanne Le Franc

II. The building now known as Calvin House

in restraining the violence of the king of France (Henri II) that he has never more boldly insulted God.'[1] Later he goes into detail in a letter addressed to an unknown person: 'Someone writes to tell me, amongst other things, what a strange sight it is to see in the ruins of our city my father's house alone left standing amid the rest reduced to ashes.' And he adds: 'I have no doubt that God wished to leave behind this witness against all those in our town who eight or ten days previously burnt an effigy of Monsieur de Normandie and the rest.'[2]

Having thus survived this fire, Calvin's house was perhaps the one that was shown at the beginning of the twentieth century as containing the room in which the Reformer was born. But this house was destroyed in 1918 during shelling and only one oaken balustrade of the ancient staircase was preserved. On the site of the ruins of this house, the present Calvin House was built in 1930, the building which at the present moment keeps alive the memory of the Reformer in his native town, and which has become a museum and a library through the care of the Society for French Protestant History.

Gérard Cauvin had seven children from his first marriage with Jeanne Le Franc,—Charles, John, Anthony, two who died very young, another Anthony and Francis,—and two daughters by a second wife whose name is not known. Anthony accompanied his brother, John, to Geneva and was his faithful collaborator. His life was saddened by the misconduct of his wife whom he finally divorced. For the Reformer the accompanying scandal was great and his grief immense. Anthony was the sole heir of his brother, who left him a silver cup which Guillaume de Trie had

[1] *Op. Calv.* XIV, Letter 1674.
[2] *Ibid.*, Letter 1704. Laurent de Normandie, the king's lieutenant, had left Noyon and taken refuge with Calvin in Geneva in 1549.

given him. His half-sister Mary came also with her brothers to Geneva and married there. The other half-sister remained at Noyon where she became the mother of a family. The elder brother, Charles, had unpleasant dealings of a very serious nature with the chapter at Noyon, exactly as his father had done. After quarrels which reached the stage of blows with a cantor, he was excommunicated and roundly declared 'that he cared little for such excommunications'. But, if we may believe the canon of Noyon, Jacques Levasseur, quoted by Drelincourt,[1] 'he absorbed and sowed the errors of his brother, sang mass and mocked it, refused the sacraments, notably the holy elements on his deathbed, and was finally buried beneath a gibbet.' There, then, is a brother of Calvin who remained at Noyon, yet who separated himself from the church and was considered a heretic and an evildoer. Drelincourt concludes: 'If in revulsion at this fine confession and this Christian resolve they buried the body of this blessed man in a place where evildoers were executed, this was for him great honour and glory.'

Undoubtedly the unpleasant proceedings of Gérard Cauvin and the canons of Noyon could scarcely have disposed his children to respect the church whose cathedral stretched its shadow across the town.[2]

---

[1] Drelincourt: *Défense de Calvin* (Geneva, 1667), pp. 237 ff.

[2] On these details see Jacques Pannier: *L'Enfance et la Jeunesse de Jean Calvin. Ses études, sa conversion, ses voyages en France (1509–1535)* (Toulouse, 1909).

CHAPTER II

CALVIN THE STUDENT

AT the age of fourteen John was sent by his father to
Paris to continue his studies there. The plague was
raging at that time in Noyon and it was as much
to protect his son from this scourge as to give him better
teaching that Gérard Cauvin took this decision. The boy
lodged with his uncle Richard, a locksmith, who lived
near Saint-Germain-l'Auxerrois. The Montmor brothers
had accompanied him to Paris and their tutor was also to
supervise Calvin's studies; but the latter's memories of
this supervision were not pleasant ones.[1] The young men
entered the Collège de la Marche. There Calvin was
taught by a man to whom, as he gratefully recognized,
he owed much, a man who was to remain one of the most
famous masters of education, Maturin Cordier. In 1550,
Calvin wrote to his former teacher[2]: 'It is only right that
you too should have a share in my labours, seeing that
under your direction, when I had at the first undertaken
the course of study, I advanced at least to the point of
being able to be of some use to the church of God. When
my father sent me to Paris as a boy, having nothing but
a few scanty rudiments of the Latin language, it pleased
God that I should meet you as my tutor for a short time,
so that I should be so well trained by you in the true road

[1] He later called him a man without judgment (*homo stolidus*).
[2] *Lettre-Préface du Commentaire à la Première Epître aux Thessaloniciens,
à Maturin Cordier* (*Op. Calv.*, XIII, p. 529).

and in the right way of learning that afterwards I might be able to profit by it. For although you had charge of the first class and taught in it with great honour, nevertheless, because you could see that children, when formed by other teachers prompted by ambition and mere bravado, were not soundly based and achieved nothing of real worth, but had merely a few whiffs of knowledge to put on some sort of show so that you had to begin all over again to fashion them anew, being angry at having to take so much trouble over the matter, you came down yourself that particular year to deal with the fourth class. . . . To have such a beginning in my education was for me a singular blessing from God. And although I was not permitted to enjoy this for long, because a scatter-brained fellow without any discretion, who controlled our studies as he wished (or rather as his mad imagination dictated) made us forthwith go up higher, nevertheless the teaching and the direction that you had given me served me so well from that time onwards that I recognize and admit, as is only just, that I had from you much of the profit and help which came later. Of this fact I have wished to bear testimony to those who shall come after us, so that, if my writings are of any use to them, they may know that this is in part due to you.'

Thus Calvin traces back to Maturin Cordier his first instruction in the Latin language which he handled with such elegance. The method of his teacher corresponded to what we today call the 'direct method'. In his *Colloques* he made boys converse amongst themselves in Latin, talking of their life as schoolboys, quoting proverbs, speaking of their buying pens, books, exercise books and of their games too. Later Calvin called Maturin Cordier to Geneva in 1536, to the Collège de Rive. After a certain time spent at Neuchâtel and at Lausanne, he came back in his old age to Geneva where he was called to organize the college.

As we said above, from the Collège de la Marche Calvin passed to the Collège Montaigu through some whim of the tutor of the Montmor brothers. Of greater repute, but at the same time noted for its greater attachment to mediaeval scholastic method than the Collège de

Courtyard of Collège Montaigu in 1779

la Marche, the Collège Montaigu was at that time (1524) under the direction of Noël Béda, a great enemy of the new ideas which were already beginning to spread. Béda had instigated the condemnation of the writings of Luther and of Lefèvre d'Etaples by the Sorbonne in 1521. Later, he directed his thunderbolts against Erasmus. The Collège Montaigu was also a centre of sarcastic opposition to the thinkers who tended to favour humanism.

Rabelais puts these words into the mouth of Gargantua's tutor: 'Don't think that I have put him in that wretched hole of a college called Montaigu . . . for convicts among the Moors and the Tartars, murderers in prisons, even dogs in your own house are better treated than the louts in that college. And if I were king of Paris, devil take me if I wouldn't set fire to it and burn both the principal and the tutors who endure the sight of this inhuman treatment before their very eyes.'[1] The masters used the birch on their pupils. The food was frugal and Calvin's digestion was ruined for life after his stay there. Erasmus described life in this college in terms which were just as violent. 'I lived thirty years ago in a college in Paris where they brewed so much theology that the walls seemed impregnated with it, but I brought nothing away with me apart from scrofula and innumerable fleas. . . . The beds were so hard, the food so wretched, the religious vigils and study so burdensome that many young men who promised well at the time of their first year's stay in this college would go mad or blind or contract leprosy—that is, if they didn't die. The punishments took the form of whippings and were administered with all the harshness expected from the hand of the hangman. The principal of the college wanted to make monks of us all and in order to teach us to fast he used to deprive us completely of meat. . . .'[2]

Calvin was a great worker; he accepted this harsh discipline. Florimond de Raemond has described him at this period: 'In a lean, worn body his mind was ever alive and vigorous, prompt in repartee, bold in attack. He fasted much, even in his youth, either for his health's sake to stop the mental haze of migraines which afflicted him continually, or to gain for his mind more freedom to

[1] Rabelais: *Gargantua*, I, xxxvii.
[2] Quoted by Doumergue, I, p. 72.

write, study and to improve his memory. . . . He spoke but little. Nothing but serious remarks and remarks which went home. He was never seen amongst groups of his fellows, always retiring, of a melancholy disposition . . . sharing his thoughts with few people, not taking pleasure in any company other than that of his own thoughts, a lover of seclusion.'[1] We see him in the courts of the college, this serious, solitary student, zealous in his studies. Under the direction of a Spanish teacher whose name has not been preserved, he passed rapidly from grammar to dialectic. His writings contain a host of quotations which indicate the wide reading which he undertook at that time: Peter Lombard, the '*Maître des Sentences*', the great author who was ceaselessly expounded by the masters of theology, St. Bernard and St. Augustine.[2] At the beginning of 1528, when he was nineteen, he became *licencié ès arts* after four years of study. The moment had arrived to choose his course of advanced studies.

Gérard Cauvin had at first destined his son for the priesthood and had directed him towards theology, but he had later changed his mind and preferred to set his course towards law. His unpleasant proceedings with the chapter of Noyon certainly counted for much in this decision. He thought, too, that the career of a lawyer would be a surer way to riches and honours for his son. Be that as it may, he found in the latter an obedient child and John went to Orleans, whose university had at that time eight professors of law, while at Paris only canon law was taught. At Orleans the most celebrated teacher was Pierre de l'Estoile,

[1] Florimond de Raemond: *Histoire de la Naissance, Progrès et Décadence de l'Hérésie de ce Siècle* (1623), VII, x, p. 885.
[2] Cf. Luchesius Smits, *St. Augustin dans l'Oeuvre de Jean Calvin* (1957). The author has discovered in the Reformer's writings 1,700 actual quotations from St. Augustine and 2,400 references, a fact which shows an extremely thorough acquaintance with Augustine's work.

later president of the Parlement de Paris and father to the famous chronicler of the reigns of Henri III and Henri IV.

At Orleans Calvin met a man who had a great influence on him, the 'Lutheran' Melchior Wolmar.[1] At the time that the young law student made his acquaintance in 1528, Wolmar had a boarder in his house, a young nine-year old nobleman, Theodore Beza. Perhaps it was at this very time that those who later were to become so deeply united in friendship first met. Others became his friends too at Orleans; François Daniel, to whom in 1530 he wrote the first letter of his immense correspondence which has been preserved, and also Nicolas Duchemin, whose lodging he shared for some time at Orleans. Calvin always remained faithful to these friends of his youth, and right up to the closing days of his life he could renew friendly relations with his earliest fellow pupils.

At the time when Calvin entered it, the University of Orleans had three to four thousand students, who were grouped in ten 'nations', that is, corporations according to their provinces or countries of origin. Each nation elected its procurator or president, as we should say today. Calvin was elected procurator for the nation of Picardie, which showed the confidence which his fellow countrymen had in their young friend, scarcely twenty years old.

Among the professors of the University of Orleans we must note Nicolas Bérauld, the teacher of the three Châtillon brothers, Gaspard de Coligny, Odet de Châtillon and François, whose characters he was able to fashion so nobly; Anne Du Bourg, professor in civil law at Orleans about 1550, counsellor of the Parlement of Paris in 1557, burnt as a heretic on the Place de Grève in 1559 on account

[1] Jean-Melchior Rot, known as Wolmar, was born at Rottweil in Wurtemberg in 1496.

23

of his energetic protest against the tortures decreed against the evangelicals: 'It is no matter of small importance to condemn those who call upon the name of Jesus Christ amid the flames'; François Hotman, an eminent, Reformed legal expert who has been accounted one of the precursors of international law, and above all Melchior Wolmar. The importance of the latter's influence upon Calvin has been mentioned above. He was certainly the centre of a little group in which Lutheran ideas were welcomed and he was doubtless the first man to unfold to Calvin the ways of the gospel.

This was an age of much travel, and after the learned discoveries of the archive hunters, we must admit that, although Calvin established his base at Orleans from 1528 until 1533, he moved about freely during this time and went from there to Bourges, Paris and Noyon. In May 1533, he was designated a substitute of the procurator of the nation of Picardie at the University of Orleans for that year, and among the names of those who signed with him we find Laurent de Normandie, also from Noyon (later lieutenant to the king) who came to Geneva in 1549, one of the faithful friends of the Reformer. But though he remained several years registered at Orleans in order to obtain his degrees of bachelor of law, licentiate (1532) and doctor (1533), in the intervening years he left this university for that of Bourges.

In 1529, Marguerite de Navarre,[1] Duchess of Berry and a friend of the humanists, had called the Italian jurist Alciat to the University of Bourges which had been

[1] The 'Marguerite des Marguerites', sister of Francis I, was thus Marguerite of Angoulême, Duchess of Alençon by her first marriage with Charles Duke of Alençon, Duchess of Berry by gift of the king, and Queen of Navarre by her second marriage with Henri d'Albret, King of Navarre. She was the mother of Jeanne d'Albret and grandmother of Henri IV.

founded by Louis XI. A certain rivalry arose between Orleans and Bourges, between Pierre de l'Estoile and Alciat. One of Calvin's friends, Nicolas Duchemin, even wrote a defence of the former legal expert, against the latter in his *Antapologia adversus Aurelii Albucii Defensionem pro Alciato contra Stellam* (A Refutation of the Defence of Aurele Albucius in favour of Alciat against Pierre de l'Estoile). Calvin supervised the publication of this small book at Paris and introduced it by letter to François de Connan in 1531. He had therefore remained more attached to l'Estoile than to Alciat, but his questing mind had spurred him on to follow in person the lectures of this new master at Bourges. There he again met Melchior Wolmar, whom Marguerite de Navarre had also attracted to her university to teach Greek, and he continued with him the conversations about evangelical doctrine which had been begun at Orleans.

Florimond de Raemond roundly asserted that Wolmar was the first to give Calvin 'the taste for heresy'. Here is what he says: '[At Bourges] he found Melchior Wolmar, quietly settled in the state of the Queen of Navarre, an unhappy and disastrous meeting. Melchior was a German, a man of great learning, a reader of Greek and a practised linguist. He was also the guide of Calvin's successor in his youth [Theodore Beza]. Having recognized in this young man [Calvin] an agile mind, a good memory and an outstanding ability to seize a point swiftly and accurately, and to profit from the lectures and suggestions which arose out of the oral disputations of his teachers—which he was afterwards able to couch in writing of amazing clarity and beauty, showing at every turn flashes of wit and pungent retorts—Wolmar attracted him to himself and favoured him above all his fellows. While walking with him one day and reasoning with him on the direction of his future career, he advised him to devote himself to theology, the queen of all the sciences, and to leave the code of Justinien for the gospel of Jesus Christ. ... Wolmar disclosed to him some of the secrets of Lutheranism, for he belonged to this sect, although he played the part of a good Catholic. ... [When Calvin left for Noyon] Wolmar kept in touch with him by letter, sent him books which he used to receive from Germany and begged Calvin to continue his venture of adorning the Church of the Lord. Calvin often admitted that this Wolmar was the man who drove him to the high achievement of his later venture.'[1]

We cannot doubt that there was an influence prior to that of Wolmar upon Calvin assisting him to understand the evangelical message. But the Roman Catholic author goes too far when he puts into the mind of Wolmar this plan to drive Calvin to an enterprise of reformation. We need no other proof than the preface to the Second Epistle to the Corinthians in which Calvin dedicates his commentator's work to Wolmar in terms which admittedly betray affectionate gratitude, but which do not however attribute to him a leading part in setting the new direction which the young lawyer's activities were to take.

Here is this letter of dedication:

'To Melchior Wolmar Roux, legal expert and most worthy man, John Calvin, greetings. If you wish to accuse me not only of negligence but also of incivility because I have written you no letter for so long a time, I confess that I can only excuse myself with great difficulty, for if I put the case that there is a long distance between us[2] and that for the space of five whole years I have met no-one who was going in that direction, the excuse would be quite true. But in myself I already recognize that it would

---

[1] Florimond de Raemond: *Op. cit.*, p. 882.
[2] Wolmar was at Tübingen at the time.

be too weak an excuse. Yet it seemed to me that there was no better way than to introduce myself with some gift in my hand, a gift which would redress the faults of time past and would achieve my reconciliation all at once. Here then is the commentary on the Second Epistle of St. Paul to the Corinthians written and drawn up by me with the greatest care and skill that I could muster. I am sending it to you now for this purpose. For I have no doubt that your generosity will accept it as sufficient recompense, although there are of course other and greater reasons which led me to dedicate it to you. First, I remember with what affection you fostered and advanced this beginning of our long friendship, how you were ready freely to use your energy and your influence on my behalf when you thought that an opportunity arose to show your love for me, how you offered me your reputation to help me on, if the calling that I was then following had not prevented me from accepting it.[1] But there is nothing so pleasant for me as the remembrance of these early times when, though sent by my father to learn civil law, I added to the study of law Greek language and literature with you as guide and teacher, subjects which you were teaching at that time and in which you stood in such high repute. And indeed it was no fault of yours that I did not profit more from this teaching, for of your kindness you were ready to lend me a helping hand until I had completed the course of study and surveyed it from start to finish. And this I should have done, had it not been for the intervention of my father's death, which was the cause of my being drawn in another direction when I had

---

[1] Thus, far from driving him in the direction of theology (as de Raemond maintains), Wolmar would have used his influence to further Calvin's progress in literary studies, though at the time he was studying law in obedience to his father's wishes.

not been long started. The fact remains, nevertheless, that I recognize my great indebtedness to you. At the very least I am grateful for the rudiments I learned under you and which have helped me since then. This is why I could find no better way to fulfil my desire than to leave to posterity a testimony that I was not willing to be considered ungrateful to you.'[1]

To this letter of 1546, Wolmar replied by sending a silver cup to the Reformer. These are friendly relations but not indications that the professor at Bourges could claim to be a spiritual father where Calvin was concerned. Two other letters from Calvin to Wolmar tell us no more. So we must abandon the suggestion of Florimond de Raemond. This was the conclusion to which Abel Lefranc had arrived in his study on the young Calvin.[2]

Nevertheless, it is at Bourges that, according to tradition, we should place Calvin's first evangelical preaching. In a street there one can still see a kind of half tower set in the wall of an ancient Augustinian convent. This is said to be the outer projection of Calvin's pulpit, from which he taught rhetoric. From this convent came Augustine Marlorat, prior of the Augustinians, who was converted to the faith of the Reformation in 1533, became a minister, and died a martyr at Rouen in 1561. To him we owe the first two published indices following the Institutes in 1568, and the prayers sometimes printed after each of Marot's and Beza's psalms, as well as numerous biblical commentaries.[3] There is also shown a *pierre à Calvin* (a 'Calvin

[1] *Op. Calv.*, XII, p. 365.
[2] A. Lefranc: *Op. cit.*, p. 39.
[3] Germain Colladon, later Calvin's secretary and a learned lawyer, also came from Bourges. Before 1550 evangelical services were being held in his house. In 1550 he left Bourges with his brother Leon (also a lawyer) and they both settled with their families at Geneva. His nephew, Nicolas Colladon, minister of Vandoeuvres in 1553, was Rector of the Academy in 1564 and Professor of Theology. In 1563 he published a *Vie de Calvin*, completing Beza's work (*Op. Calv.*, XXI, pp. 51-118).

stone') at the fishmarket in the Place Gordaine, on to which Calvin is said to have climbed to preach to the crowd, like the one shown at Montbéliard in the market-place as having been used by the Reformer Pierre Toussain. Between Bourges and the neighbouring village of Asnières, even until quite recently, tradition pointed out a bridge (since carried away by floods) which used to be known as Calvin's bridge, in memory of the preaching which the future Reformer is said to have given in this village—a village which has remained since the sixteenth century very much attached to Protestantism. Theodore Beza speaks also of a sermon at the village of Lignières, preached with the approval of the lord of the district who was also lord of Meillant. From here the letter to François Daniel in 1530 was written.

In 1531 Gérard Cauvin died. His son had left Bourges and had joined him at Noyon. His father's illness kept him back some time but all hope of cure had to be given up and after two months of suffering the end came. At the bedside of his dying father Calvin wrote his friend, Nicolas Duchemin, a letter to apologize for his long silence and to explain the reason for it. This letter his adversaries have sometimes quoted when wishing to blame him for lack of softer feelings. We ought rather to speak of an extreme reserve in showing his deepest feelings. The death of Gérard Cauvin had a profound influence on the direction of his son's life. He was freed from the responsibility to his father as far as his lawyer's career was concerned. He could now follow his deepest conviction as to his true calling, the conviction which had, we believe, been present for some years. It was the call to become a theologian.

CHAPTER III

CALVIN THE HUMANIST[1]

IT is not, however, as a theologian that the twenty-five-year-old student first rose to prominence, but as a humanist. Leaving Bourges and Noyon he settled in Paris at the Collège Fortet on the Sainte-Geneviève hill, opposite the Collège Montaigu where he had formerly spent several years.[2] Francis I had just founded the college of royal lectors which was later to become the Collège de France. Guillaume Budé, who had restored Greek studies to the syllabus and a man whom Theodore Beza placed in his gallery of *Icones, or True Portraits of Men Famed for their Piety and their Doctrine*, had obtained from the king the statutes of this college which was intended to be opposed to the narrowness and the obscurantism of the Sorbonne. He is said to have wanted Erasmus as Principal, but after some hesitation, the latter refused. Budé brought Pierre Danès and Jacques Toussain to teach Greek. For Hebrew there was François Vatable, who taught this language to the future translator of the Psalms, Clément Marot. Calvin, who had studied Greek under Melchior

---

[1] The relation of Calvin to the humanism of the early 16th century has been studied by J. Bohatec in his book *Budé und Calvin* (1950). See also Imbart de la Tour, *Les Origines de la Réforme* (1914), III; J. Plattard, *Guillaume Budé et les Origines de l'Humanisme française*, (1923).

[2] The city of Paris has given Calvin's name to a recently-made street at the bottom of Rue Tournefort, only a short distance away in the centre of the University quarter.

Wolmar, continued to study it under Danès. But he devoted himself especially to Latin. In 1532 he published a commentary on the *De Clementia* of Seneca which he dedicated to his fellow pupil, Claude de Hangest, Abbot of Saint-Eloi at Noyon.

This treatise begins with a short life of Seneca. It then gives the text of the work, virtually as Erasmus had established it in 1529, and a line-by-line commentary, all with great linguistic erudition. According to the judgment of Jacques Pannier 'this is a valuable product of a serious student taking an interest in what he is doing and awake to all that is going on in both the world of letters and in contemporary affairs . . . but if he had not become a famous Reformer his commentary would have been completely forgotten.'[1]

It is true that the treatise of Seneca deserved a thorough study. A recent commentator has shown that it played a not inconsiderable part in French literature. 'It provided Montaigne with the model of a story which was lively and colourful as well as edifying; it provided Corneille with the subject of one of his masterpieces: and Racine with the fine tirades of Burrhus which give an especially noble quality to the play *Britannicus*.'[2] Many have thought that Calvin's intention in choosing to produce a commentary on this particular text was to provoke clemency for the cause of all those who were being persecuted for their faith, imprisoned and burned as heretics. On April 16, 1529 Louis de Berquin, a nobleman of Picardy and translator of some writings of Luther and Erasmus, was burned on the Place de Grève. Some have thought that even at

[1] J. Pannier: 'Research on the evolution of Calvin's religion up to his conversion', *Revue d'Histoire et de Philosophie religieuse* (Strasbourg, 1923), p. 209.

[2] F. Préhac: *Sénèque: De la Clémence*, Editions Guillaume Budé.

this early date Calvin was considering appealing to Francis I, giving him to understand through the voice of the ancient philosopher what he was later to say in his prefatory letter to the *Institutes*: 'You have to consider of your *clemency* and gracious condescension that there would be no innocence left at all, either in word or deed, if mere accusation were enough.' But is not this going too far in the realm of conjecture? In actual fact there is no allusion to contemporary events in the young student's commentary, which is purely philological, historical and above all legal. Perhaps the most important point to be noted about this first work is that it was an unsuccessful attempt by Calvin towards a literary career and towards humanism, following in the footsteps of Budé and Erasmus. The small success that this tentative effort met with, the lack of enthusiasm on the part of his teachers and his equals, the difficulty of meeting the expenses of printing, in a word, the disappointment which is felt behind the words of a letter such as the one he wrote to his friend Daniel[1] at this juncture—these considerations may well have been of some importance in closing for Calvin the road of secular philology and opening before him that of theology and commenting on Holy Scripture.

[1] *Op. Calv.*, X^b, p. 19.

CHAPTER IV

CALVIN'S CONVERSION

THE time has come to ask ourselves at what period Calvin took his stand on the side of evangelical views. The commentary on *De Clementia* is dated 1532. We have not been able to find any clearly theological affirmation in it. In 1533, Calvin is back in Orleans, as the date of several texts quoted above have shown. Then, in August, 1533, he is again mentioned at Noyon among the canons of the chapter who ordered public prayers against the plague and, in consequence, he must still have been in possession of the benefice from which he had profited ever since his youth. But in October, 1533, several new facts allow us to be precise about his taking a position more clearly on the side of the Reformation.

On October 1 in that year students of the Collège de Navarre in Paris performed a satirical comedy, a farce in which they attacked Master Gérard Roussel under the thinly disguised name of *Mégère*, made up of the first letters of his name: M, G, R. Neither did they spare the poetic work of Marguerite de Navarre. The second edition of her book, *Le Miroir de l'Ame pécheresse*, had just appeared, in which she recognizes her faults and sins and also the graces and blessings which have been granted to her by Jesus Christ her spouse.

Here are a few verses from this poem:

Man is by faith made son of the Creator.
Man is by faith, righteous, holy and a doer of good.

Man is by faith restored to a state of innocence.
Man is by faith a king in Christ who reigns.
By faith we have the Spirit of consolation.
United to the Father and to the Mediator.
By faith I have Christ and all things richly.

The pupils of the Collège de Navarre did not like faith being thus exalted and their sarcastic comments were directed even to the king's sister, 'Marguerite très noble et précieuse'. In a letter written to his friend, François Daniel, Calvin tells him the whole story.[1] The Queen of Navarre complained to her brother Francis I. The latter, learning that the *Miroir de l'Ame pécheresse* had been put on a list of forbidden books by some theologians, asked the teachers of the Sorbonne to give him the reasons for this step.

The rector of the University at that time was Nicolas Cop, a friend of Calvin, who had been nominated only seventeen days previously. He was the son of Guillaume Cop, the king's doctor, who was a close friend of Erasmus. On being questioned by the king he called together the four faculties—medicine, philosophy, theology and canon law—and gave them to understand that no censure could be pronounced against the queen's work.

A few days later, rector Cop was to preach a sermon in the church of the Mathurins on All Saints' Day, November 1, 1533. This sermon was something of a manifesto of evangelical ideas.[2] In the first part he describes 'Christian philosophy', the source of true and certain blessedness. It is simply that we should understand and believe that we

[1] Herminjard: *Correspondance des Réformateurs*, III, p. 106. Cf. also on these facts V. L. Bourrilly and N. Weiss: 'Jean du Bellay, les protestants et la Sorbonne', *B.H.P.F.*, 1903, pp. 193–231.

[2] The text is given in *Op. Calv.*, X$_b$, pp. 30–36; Herminjard: *Correspondance des Réformateurs*, III, pp. 418ff.

are the sons of God. This wisdom by its very glory darkens all the wisdom of the world. To bring it to us God was willing to become man, the immortal became mortal. This wisdom consists in the remission of sins solely through the grace of God. It teaches that the Holy Spirit, who sanctifies the heart and gives eternal life, is promised to all Christians. After this exordium, the sermon continues with a commentary on the Beatitudes. Here is its conclusion:

' "Blessed", says Jesus, "shall you be when for my sake men shall despise you and persecute you and say evil against you falsely!" Why should we then pretend and prefer not to tell the truth? Is it right to please men rather than God, to fear those who can destroy the body but not the soul? O ingratitude of the human race which can suffer nothing for Him who died for its sins, who by His blood has delivered us from the chains of Satan and eternal death! The world is accustomed to call those who strive to spread in the souls of men the pure gospel and believe that thus they are obeying God, heretics, seducers, imposters and slanderers. But blessed and worthy of envy are those who bear all this with serenity, blessing God amidst calamities and undergoing afflictions with great courage. "Rejoice," He says, "for your reward is great in heaven."

'Come then Christian men, let us strain our every nerve for this blessedness. God, who by His word brings to birth in all faith, hope and charity, draws us by His grace; He opens our minds so that we may believe the gospel, and so that we may understand that there is only one God who alone must be served with all our soul and in whose name we must bear all and suffer all. May He fill us with peace and joy in believing so that in hope we may be victorious in the power of the Holy Spirit and finally

35

triumph in heaven with an eternal triumph. Amen.'

This evangelical sermon was delivered from a Catholic pulpit. Its allusions to the persecutions and opposition, its reminder of the grace of God alone, its affirmation that God alone opens men's hearts and gives them faith, all this is pure Reformation doctrine. In the library at Geneva the text of the sermon has been found in Calvin's handwriting with this note from his secretary Colladon: 'Sermon written on behalf of Nicolas Cop'. It seems then that Calvin was the author of it.[1] For its opening he leans heavily on the exhortation placed by Erasmus at the beginning of his third edition of the New Testament, and for the commentary on the Beatitudes on a sermon of Luther translated into Latin by Bucer. However that may be, the rector and his friend are clearly seen here taking up a definite position.

The Parlement reacted and, as a result of a denunciation by the Franciscans, wished to have Cop and Calvin arrested. Cop fled in the direction of Basle and Calvin also made off towards Angoulême. Here, then, is a date (November 1, 1533) when there is no possibility of doubting Calvin's convictions. He has been won over to the gospel of grace, he is on the side of the persecuted and those who are suffering for their faith.

Must we go further back and date this conversion several years previously? What we have seen above of the influence of Wolmar on the young student at Orleans and what we have said about the preaching of Calvin at Bourges, Lignières and Asnières strongly incline us to this view. We believe that as early as 1529, the reading of the evangelical innovators had made some impression on him. A text of the *Second Defence against Westphal* seems to us to indicate as much:

[1] See however the reservations of Wendel: *Calvin*, p. 23.

'Beginning to emerge somewhat from the darkness of popery, and having acquired some little taste for sound doctrine, when I was reading in Luther that Œcolampadius and Zwingli left nothing in the sacraments but bare figures and symbols without the reality, I confess that that turned me from their books, so that for a long time I read none of them. Now before I began to write [and therefore before 1534, date of the *Psychopannychia* written at Orleans] they had conferred together at Marburg [in 1529] and by this means their first vehemence was a little moderated, to such an extent that although the weather was not completely set fair again, yet the thickest darkness had begun to be scattered a little.'[1]

Thus, before 1529 Calvin was reading the writings of Luther and he had even enough knowledge to judge between Luther and Zwingli in the controversies. Before 1529 then, he had already begun to come out of 'the darkness of popery'.

It may be objected that this conversion could not have been very definite since Calvin kept his ecclesiastical benefices until 1534. How can we allow that the one who was later so severe on the middle-of-the-road men, the Nicodemites as he called them, alluding to the timid visitor to Jesus by night, how can we admit that this man should have kept for several years after an inner break with the Catholic Church, a mundane connection as important as this? We reply that at that time, such benefices were universally regarded as scholarships, and were thus doubtless kept by Calvin until the end of the course of study which was to lead him to his doctorate of law in 1533, at the very time when his faith had moved far from the beliefs of his youth.

---

[1] Calvin: *Opuscules* (1566), p. 1503; *Op. Calv.*, IX, p. 51.

We believe then that the stages in Calvin's conversion can be fixed as follows:

May 4, 1534: resigns his ecclesiastical benefice.

November 1, 1533: the sermon of rector Cop.

1533: stay at Orleans.

1532: evangelical activity at Bourges.

1531: influence of humanism.

1530: the unpleasant proceedings of Gérard Cauvin and his family with the chapter of Noyon.

1529: influence of Melchior Wolmar and the reading of Lutheran books.

We can even go further back and see in 1528 a prior influence on him, that of a relation, Pierre-Robert Olivétan of Noyon. Theodore Beza said: 'Having already by means of a relation and friend of his, named M. Pierre Robert, otherwise known as Olivetanus, who has since translated the Hebrew Bible into French at Neuchâtel, tasted something of pure religion, he was beginning to see his way out of papal superstitions.'[1] There is no reason to reject this testimony given to one whom Calvin calls in his Latin preface to the Bible of 1535 'a relation and longstanding friend', and further on, 'our Robert'. Thus 'the humble and lowly translator' of holy Scripture could have been the first to open to his cousin the ways of the gospel.

Calvin was always very reticent on the details of his conversion. His sole aim to give God alone the glory led him to leave in shadow that which concerned himself personally. He considered such details as without interest. Lovers of psychology who find in the writings of our own time all too many analyses and interminable passages of introspection, are disappointed that they find in the considerable volume of the Reformer's work so little auto-

[1] *Op. Calv.*, XXI, p. 54.

biographical information. Here, however, are two fragments which must be quoted in their entirety in view of
their importance.

First in the preface to the *Commentary on the Psalms*,
dated 1558:

'Even while I was a boy my father had destined me for
theology; then, later, as he considered that the knowledge
of law commonly enriched those who followed it, this
hope made him straightway change his mind. This, then,
was why I was taken from the study of philosophy and
put to learn law, from which (although I made every
effort to use my talents faithfully in obedience to my
father) nevertheless God in His secret providence finally
curbed and turned me in another direction. At first,
although I was so obstinately given to the superstitions of
the papacy, that it was extremely difficult to drag me from
the depths of the mire, yet by a sudden conversion He
tamed my heart and made it teachable, this heart which
for its age was excessively hardened in such matters. So,
having received some taste and knowledge of true piety,
I was at once inflamed with so great a desire to advance
that, although I did not entirely leave my other studies,
yet nevertheless I was less rigorous in the way I devoted
myself to them.'

This text places the conversion or rather the calling of
Calvin during the course of his law studies. If then in
1528 Olivétan first approached his cousin with evangelical
ideas, it was not until 1529 and at the time of his first
contact with Wolmar at Orleans at the beginning of his
stay at the university, that the sudden conversion by
which God 'tamed his heart and made it teachable'
became known. Here is God laying His hand on this life
which will never in future cease to be controlled by this
sovereignty. We must note the expressions 'curb' and

'turn' and 'tame', which remind us of the words of Luther comparing himself to a blind horse led by its rider. Some biographers of Calvin have tried to translate *conversio subita* by a conversion which was experienced (*subie*), rather than a conversion which was sudden (*subite*). The two senses are possible yet not contradictory. This certainty of being laid hold of by God was from then on to dominate Calvin's whole life. Strohl sees in this experience of the living and sovereign God the characteristic emphasis of the whole Reformation movement. 'What characterizes the Reformation is not so much its protest against long-standing abuses, a protest which had been heard throughout the whole of the fifteenth century, but rather a discovery of the living God, author of all grace and of every perfect gift. None of those who were blest with the privilege of being gripped by God ever attributed the least merit to himself on this account. It was for them all a mystery of divine mercy. One cannot be surprised that these men often pursued the idea of unconditional grace to its extremest consequences, for grace, by its own sovereign initiative alone, takes hold of those whom it has chosen.'[1]

In his *Letter to Sadoletus* (1539) there is another passage which also gives us some data. Leaving the discussion with the cardinal, Calvin turns toward God, addressing Him in these magnificent phrases: 'Every time that I looked within myself, or raised my heart to Thee, so violent a horror overtook me that there were neither purifications nor satisfactions which could in any way cure me. The more I gazed at myself the sharper were the pricks which pressed my conscience, to such a point that there remained no other solace or comfort than to deceive myself by forgetting myself. But because nothing better was offered

[1] H. Strohl: *La Pensée de la Réforme* (1951), pp. 22ff.

me, I continued on the course that I had begun. Then, however, there arose a quite different form of doctrine, not to turn us away from our Christian profession but rather to bring it back to its proper source and to restore it in its purity, cleansed, as it were, from all filth. But I, offended by the newness of it, was scarcely willing to listen to a word of it and I admit that at the beginning I valiantly and courageously resisted it. For, as men are naturally obstinate and stubborn in maintaining the system that they have once received, I had to confess that all my life I had been nourished in error and ignorance. And there was one thing especially which kept me from believing these people, that was reverence for the Church. But after I had sometimes listened and suffered being taught, I realized that any such fear that the majesty of the Church might be diminished was vain and superfluous. And when my mind had been made ready to be truly attentive I began to understand, as if someone had brought me a light, in what a mire of error I had wallowed, and had become filthy, and with how much mud and dirt I had been defiled. Being then grievously troubled and distracted, as was my duty, on account of the wretched state into which I had fallen and yet more on account of the knowledge of the eternal death which hung over me, I judged nothing more necessary to me after having condemned with groaning and tears my past manner of life, than to give myself up and to betake myself to Thy way. . . .'[1]

This is an admirable passage in which Calvin confides in us more freely than in the former quotation. He reveals himself as overwhelmed by the consciousness of sin, just as Luther was, and constrained in his conscience. He tells us that his conversion was not, as has sometimes been

[1] Calvin: *Opuscules*, pp. 170ff.

maintained, a cold intellectual decision, but an act in the depths of a heart which trusts. He shows us his struggles, his hesitation in leaving the Church of his childhood, and his repentance with tears. Here is true greatness. But especially do we feel in these pages this grip of God on his life, this impossibility of resisting the heavenly vision, this 'I can do no other' which is indeed the hallmark of Reformation piety.

CHAPTER V

1534: A YEAR OF TRAVEL

THE sermon of Nicolas Cop, preached in November, 1533, had aroused a violent reaction in the Parlement of Paris. The young rector had fled to Basle to his father. Gérard Roussel, the almoner of Marguerite d'Angoulême, who became bishop of Oloron in Béarn, was arrested together with an Augustinian monk, Elias Coraud, the blind preacher, whom we shall find a few years later at Geneva with Farel. They were to be freed a short time afterwards as a result of the personal intervention of Marguerite d'Angoulême. But Francis I did not hold the same views as his sister. On December 10, 1533, he wrote the following letter from Lyons to the Parlement of Paris:

'We are very distressed and displeased that in our fair city of Paris, head and principal city of our kingdom, where stands the principal university of the whole of Christendom, this accursed, heretical, Lutheran sect should be breeding where many others might well follow its example; with all our power and might we wish to prevent this, without sparing anyone. For this reason we wish and intend that such grievous punishment shall be given to it that it shall be both a correction to the accursed heretics and an example to all the others.

'For this reason we command you and enjoin you expressly to commit some of your number in order that they may curiously and diligently enquire of all those who hold the opinions of this Lutheran sect and who are under grave suspicion on this account, and those who adhere to it and follow these beliefs, in order that you may take proceedings against them, without excepting anyone, by laying hands upon them in whatever place they may be found and by confiscating the goods of those who have fled. And as for those whom you have made prisoner, who are charged with blasphemy, proceed to their punishment according to the demands of the case.

'And with regard to the heretics, we are writing to the bishop of Paris, or to his deputies, that they should commit two of our counsellors . . . to attend to and carry through their proceedings . . . , seeing that this criminal sect is rapidly multiplying for lack of our having taken care to root it out at the very beginning. . . .'[1]

Thus Francis I had decided to fight against the Evangelicals as early as 1533. Calvin, warned by the flight of Cop, swiftly left his room in the Collège Fortet; one account even has it that he escaped through the window and slipped out of Paris in the borrowed clothes of a vine-dresser, with beggar's sack on back and hoe on shoulder.[2] He then made his way to Noyon and thence into Saintonge.

Then one of his friends, Louis Du Tillet, invited him to move to Angoulême. Louis was parish priest at Claix and canon of the cathedral, and belonged to a family of scholars and public servants. There Calvin found a friendly welcome awaiting him. He was happy working in a long gallery in which he found three or four thousand books and manuscripts. Calvin spent several months in this learned retreat. About March, 1534, he wrote from Orleans to his friend Daniel:

'The only thing which might interest you for the

[1] Herminjard: *Correspondance des Réformateurs*, III, pp. 115 ff.
[2] Doumergue: *Calvin*, I, p. 354.

moment is that I am in good health and, considering my laziness of which you know, I am making progress in my studies. Certainly the kindness of my patron is so great that it is addressed, I well understand this, to literature rather than to me personally, and would soften the most insensitive man. I should consider myself very happy if I am allowed to spend this time of exile or retreat in such tranquillity. But the Lord will do what pleases Him, His providence will see what is best. I have learnt by experience that we are not allowed to see too much of the future. While I was promising myself that I would be quiet, the danger of which I had no fear at all was at the gates.[1] And on the other hand, when I feared that my stay would be a frightful one, a nest has been prepared for me in quietness, contrary to all expectation, and it is the hand of God that has done all this. If we trust in Him, He will watch over us Himself.'[2]

The tone of absolute confidence and peace is indeed the sign that Calvin had already a profound faith in the sovereignty of God, very different from the earlier letters that he used to write to Daniel.

What was the work of this 'notorious lazy bones' who devoted a portion of his nights to study? Florimond de Raemond tells us: 'Angoulême was the forge in which this new Vulcan fashioned on the anvil the strange opinions which he has since published. For it was there that, to surprise Christendom, he first wove the tapestry of his *Institutes*, this book that one may call the Koran or rather the Talmud of heresy.'[3] A group of lettered men and humanists quickly formed around Calvin. As he

[1] An allusion to the searches in the Collège Fortet.
[2] Herminjard: *Ibid.*, III, p. 156. Translation in Doumergue: *Op. cit.*, pp. 371-372.
[3] Florimond de Raemond: *Op. cit.*, p. 883.

taught Greek (which was still little known) to his friend
the priest of Claix, they called him 'the Greek of Claix'.
'So, in high esteem and repute, beloved by all those who
loved literary scholarship, he wove into his lectures statements about religion, and was always ready to let fly some
pointed allusion against the authority of the traditions of
the Church. He was soon supported by several people in
authority: Antoine Chaillou, prior of Bouteville (whom
they soon called "the pope of the Lutherans"), and also
the abbot of Bassac, both lettered men, keen to collect all
the good books that could be got; the lord of Torsac and
his brother, Pierre De La Place.[1] Calvin was often found
in their company. Their meeting-place was a house just
outside the town of Angoulême named Girac, where the
prior of Bouteville usually lived. There he discussed with
them the plans for his *Institutes*, opening to them all the
secrets of his theology, reading chapters from his book as
he wrote them, and so zealous at this work that he often
spent entire nights without sleeping and days without
eating.'[2]

'Calvin stayed for a few years in the town of Angoulême,'
continues our author in a later passage, 'still wearing
outwardly the mask of a Catholic, being present at church
but as seldom as possible. He was employed by the chapter
to deliver the Latin narrations as was the custom when
the synod assembled, which task he performed three times
in St. Peter's Church. During the time he stayed in
Angoulême, he engaged in no religious practice which was
anti-catholic, nor in any preaching nor praying. He was
not used to these yet and all these discussions with these

---

[1] *Translator's note.* Distinguished lawyer and historian, converted
to the Reformation about 1560. He died in the massacre of St. Barth
olomew, 1572.
[2] *Ibid.*, p. 884.

three good churchmen (Du Tillet, the prior of Bouteville and the abbot of Bassac) was simply in the style of a disputation seeking the truth, an expression which was normally on his lips when he opened any book; "Let us find the truth", he would say.'[1]

Thus, thanks to the Catholic pamphleteer, we can glimpse some features of this period when Calvin was pursuing in solitude the studies and researches from which the *Institutes* were to come. It was a period of gestation and private re-thinking, as also of stubborn toil in search of the truth; an uncertain period in which the young theologian drew up sermons for the local priests at a time when he had already in his heart broken with the Catholic Church. Several have reproached Calvin for this attitude, in which they see a lack of resolve; but this is to misconceive the seriousness, not to say the impossibility, of this break. Now, in the light of our present ideas, we are able to judge the matter, for we have a knowledge of two Christian Confessions clearly established, each having their own worship, doctrine and ceremonies and between which a fully enlightened choice can be made, though still not without a struggle on occasions. But in 1534, there was in France no form of evangelical Church. This was to be set up some twenty years later. Lutheran ideas had spread in certain monasteries, certain scholarly circles, certain secret academies, such as the one which met in the country house at the gates of Angoulême, or in 'the bookshop' of Louis Du Tillet. There had been martyrs at the stake. But to leap out of the only Church then established was almost unthinkable. Let us not speak of any mask, or of conspiracy, or of clandestine planning but rather of a passionate search for the truth and of conversations

[1] *Ibid.*, p. 889. All this information is confirmed by Beza: *Op. Calv.* XXI, p. 56.

47

such as men have before whom new roads are opening through the study of the gospel.[1]

In April, 1534, Calvin went to Nérac, the little capital of Albret in which Marguerite of Angoulême, sister of Francis I, Queen of Navarre and mother of Jeanne d'Albret, welcomed humanists and Evangelicals, those who were threatened by the unyielding policy of the Sorbonne and of the Parlement. Nérac had become the land of refuge for these outlaws. Gérard Roussel celebrated his 'seven-point mass' there. Here are its main features:

1. The mass will be said by the priest in the customary manner with the same ritual but there will be compulsory public communion.

2. There will be no elevation of the host.

3. There will be no adoration of the host.

4. The priest and the faithful will communicate in both kinds, with bread and with wine.

5. During the sacrifice there will be no commemoration of the virgin or of the saints.

6. The communion will be made with ordinary bread in the manner of the Greek church, the priest will break the bread on the altar, will eat part of it and distribute the remainder to the people.

7. The priests will not be bound by the vow of celibacy.[2]

The queen was ardently in favour of evangelical doctrine. This was not the taste of her husband, Henri d'Albret and sometimes it used to get to the point of

[1] Calvin's short stay at Angoulême has left a few more or less legendary traces. Calvin's vine, which Drelincourt knew in 1667, is still shown, as is Calvin's pulpit, Calvin's room and Calvin's caves; the latter are excavations in the chalk cliffs on the outskirts of the town without any real connection with the one whom later tradition liked to picture as a hunted man, hiding in the country and preaching secretly.

[2] Florimond de Raemond: *Op cit.*, p. 854.

annoying him. 'One day', wrote Jeanne d'Albret, 'this happened when the queen was praying in her room with ministers Roussel and Farel, who slipped out greatly agitated; the king, my honoured father, fetched her a slap on the right cheek and had me beaten, forbidding me roughly to meddle with doctrines.'[1]

At Nérac, Calvin wished above all to meet an old man, Jacques Lefèvre d'Etaples (*Faber Stapulensis*), former professor in the college of cardinal Lemoine whose commentaries on the Psalms in 1509, and on the Epistles of St. Paul in 1512, had pioneered the track that Reformed exegesis was to take. In this year, 1534, there had appeared at Anvers the translation of the whole Bible under the title: *The Holy Bible in French, translated according to the pure and complete translation of Jerome, compared and entirely revised according to the oldest and most accurate copies.* The first edition of this revision, of which we may say that it is the first translation of the Bible in French, dates from 1530, five years before the translation of Olivétan which appeared in Serrières near Neuchâtel, at the printing-house of Pierre de Wingle in 1535. We may guess what took place at the meeting between this fine old man and the young man, one aged eighty, the other twenty-five; the one, despite his biblical and theological knowledge, had never dared to break openly with the papacy, the other was on the point of making this final break.

A curious tale which Marguerite d'Angoulême told to Frederick II, the Elector Palatine, in a discussion which they had in Paris in 1538, gives us an insight into the thought of the old man:

'Old Jacques Lefèvre of Etaples in Picardy, who was one of the most learned men of his century, finding himself at the time persecuted in Paris by those of the Sor-

[1] Quoted by Marc Forissier: *Nérac, Ville royale et huguenote*, p. 41.

bonne, withdrew to Nérac to Marguerite, Queen of Navarre. The princess, who loved letters, received this fine old man joyfully and often discussed with him deep and serious matters. One day having decided to dine with him she brought with her a number of learned people. During the meal the old man appeared very sad and sometimes even shed tears. The queen, having noticed this, asked him the reason, jestingly reproaching him for showing sadness instead of contributing to the general entertainment. "Alas, madam", the old man replied to her, "how could I be joyful or contribute to the joy of others being the most evil man on earth." "What sin can you have committed," replied the queen, "you who seem to have led from your earliest days so holy and innocent a life?" "Madam, I find myself at the age of 101[1] without ever having touched a woman and I do not remember that I have ever committed any fault with which my conscience may be charged when I leave the world, unless it be one single fault which I believe cannot be expiated." The queen having pressed him to reveal it to her, the old man replied weeping, "Madam, how can I stand before the judgment of God? I have taught the gospel in all its purity to so many people, who have themselves suffered death for it, yet I have always avoided death, even in an age in which far from needing to fear it I ought rather to desire it." [2] He was comforted by the queen and he died very peacefully the following night.

According to Florimond de Raemond, 'Lefèvre went farther [than his disciple Gérard Roussel] in the opinions of Calvin, whom he wished however to hold back for fear

[1] This figure seems to be incorrect. According to *France Protestante*, Lefèvre was born in 1455 and died in 1537. He was therefore aged 82.

[2] E. Doumergue: *Op. cit.*, I, pp. 402, 403. The story has been contested by Bayle (in his article 'Fèvre' in the *Dictionnaire philosophique*) but without reason. It is confirmed by Farel.

that this fiery spirit might cause a general disorder; in departing he counselled him to fashion his own opinions on the model of those of Melanchthon.'[1]

Calvin's Pulpit at Nérac

Calvin remained at Nérac only a short time. In May, 1534, he went to Noyon, there to give up his ecclesiastical benefices. He was then twenty-five years of age, the age at which he could be ordained priest. Would he be like Briçonnet, like Michel d'Arande, like Gérard Roussel, like Du Tillet, a humanist prelate striving to preach the evangelical doctrines without breaking with the Catholic Church? No, Calvin had already made the final break, several years previously. He was now to bring it into the full light of day by renouncing his benefices in the chapel of la Gésine and the parish of Pont-l'Evêque. This resignation took place on May 4. On May 6, judicial proceedings were begun by

[1] *Op. cit.*, p. 922.

the chapter against his brother, Charles Cauvin. Was not this the proof that, for the chapter at Noyon, the Cauvin family, John as well as Charles, were heretics and that they were to be dealt with seriously?

In September, 1534, Calvin wrote from Noyon to Martin Bucer at Strasbourg.[1] This letter begins by the traditional greeting of the Evangelicals: 'Grace and peace from the Lord be with you by the mercy of God and the victory of Christ.' Calvin recommends to Bucer a 'brother' unjustly set aside under suspicion of anabaptism. He speaks here of brothers and friends, expressions which seem to show that already at Noyon there was a little group which formed a secret evangelical community.

Still in this same year we find Calvin at Paris. He had arranged a meeting there with a young Spanish doctor, Michael Servetus, who had just published a small book on *The Errors of the Trinity* (at Haguenau in 1531), a book in which for the first time since Arius the divinity of Christ was attacked. Calvin knew that Paris was a dangerous place for him to stay and that there was a risk that he might be arrested there. However, he offered Servetus a discussion in the presence of several other people in a house in rue Saint-Antoine. Servetus accepted the appointment but did not come to it.

Pursuing his way towards the south-west, Calvin then went to Poitiers. Florimond de Raemond, with his customary exactitude, which we have no reason to doubt, whatever Bayle may say,[2] tells us that in this town a circle of friends rapidly formed around the young man. These friends used to meet in the garden of the lieutenant-general, in the rue des Basses-Treilles. 'As our first fathers

[1] We follow the date given by Herminjard: *Correspondance*, III, p. 201.

[2] Bayle: *Dictionnaire historique et critique*, article 'Calvin', note AA.

were first bewitched and deceived in a garden, so in this garden in the rue des Basses-Treilles, this handful of men were flattered and duped by Calvin. For although he did not possess the grace or felicity of fair speech that he had in fair writing, he easily made a breach in the soul of those who would listen to him, bringing much vehemence into his talk, although by fits and starts. Here the first Calvinist council was held', says Florimond de Rae-mond.[1] The principal subject of these discussions was the presence of Christ in the Lord's Supper. Here too, according to the same author, the first Calvinist service was held in some hidden locality, caves or grottos. 'There, Calvin gave the exhortation (that was what they called preaching at first), calling on the Holy Spirit that He might descend on this little flock assembled in His Name. He would read some chapter of Scripture and immediately they would clear up, or rather muddle up their difficulties. Each one used to give his own opinion as they would at a private disputation.'[2]

One day when a discussion had arisen on the Lord's Supper, according to the same author, 'Calvin having his Bible before him said, "Here is my mass." And, throwing the hood of his cloak on to the table and raising his eyes to heaven, he exclaimed, "Lord, if on the day of judgment you hold it against me that I never went to mass and that I left it, I shall say and with reason, Lord, you did not command it. Here is your law, here is Scripture which is the rule you have given me, in which I have not been able to find any sacrifice other than that which was offered on the altar of the cross." '[3]

[1] *Op. cit.*, p. 892.
[2] *Ibid.*, p. 893. Behind the sarcastic remarks of the Catholic author we can discern the picture of an informal gathering for worship and mutual edification.
[3] *Ibid.*, p. 906.

And here, still from the same source, is how they celebrated the first services of the Lord's Supper: 'In caves and hidden places at the very beginning they introduced a form of communion called manducation, a ceremony they got from Calvin, who led his first group of enlightened followers into the caves of Crotelles. . . . One in the company, elected by them,[1] would read such a passage from the four Gospels as seemed good to him on the subject of the sacrament of the Eucharist, and having expressed his detestation of the mass as an invention of the devil he would say to them, "Brethren let us eat the bread of the Lord in memory of His death and passion." Then they would sit down to the table, then he would break the bread and give to each of them a piece and all would eat together without saying a word, each putting on the best face that he could. They did the same when they took the wine, after which this elected representative would give thanks to the Lord for His favour towards them in allowing them to recognize the abuses of papacy and in granting grace to understand the truth. This done, he would say with the others the Lord's Prayer and the creed in Latin; then the assembly would rise.'[2] We may thus regard Poitiers as the place of origin of Reformed worship.

Also in this year, 1534, Calvin wrote his first theological treatise, dated from Orleans as the Preface tells us. The title of it is *Psychopannychia*. This word signifies 'the watch of souls'.[3] The sub-title explains the title in the following lines: 'A treatise in which it is proved that souls are awake and live after they have left the body, against the error of

[1] Chosen and nominated by the others, hence their pastor. This reminds us of the description of the Lord's Supper in the middle of the second century in Justin Martyr's *Apology*.

[2] *Ibid.*, p. 910.

[3] From *psyche*, soul, and *pannychizo*, to remain awake throughout the night. This treatise was recently re-edited by Zimmerli, Leipzig, 1932.

some ignorant people who think that they sleep until the last judgment.' Although written in 1534 the treatise was not published until 1542. This was a Latin version. Not until 1558 did it appear in French.

We may be astonished that Calvin's first religious writing bears on a rather obscure question. But we must remember that the 'ignorant people' whose error he wished to combat were the Anabaptists whose heresies were causing great agitation in the popular mind. We are on the eve of the great tragedy of the siege of Munster (1535). Throughout Europe the term Anabaptist was synonymous for a revolutionary, dangerous agitator, a destroyer of the established order and accepted doctrines. It was absolutely necessary that the Reformation movement that was coming into being in France should be distinguished from these fanatics who had drawn so much popular opposition against themselves. Here are a few lines from the Preface which is marked by the characteristic style of the Reformer.

'Although a few good people had long requested, nay, urged me to write something to check the madness of those who foolishly and stupidly dispute today on the sleep or the death of the soul, hitherto I have not been able to accede to their prayers and urgent requests, as my mind is so set against all contention and dispute. And indeed I had then good reason to excuse myself, partly because I hoped that these fantastic opinions, finding no adherents, would shortly fade away, or would simply remain hidden in a host of empty chatterboxes; partly also because it was not easy for me to enter into battle against adversaries whose army, weapons, ambushes I did not yet know. For I had not then heard of them apart from a few confusedly mumbled things, so that in wanting to fight men who had not yet come out into open country, I could only look like a man beating the air with his eyes closed. But the outcome has proved quite other than I hoped, for these babblers have been so careful and diligent to increase their sect that they have already attracted to their error quite several thousand persons. From what I can see the evil has even been made worse, for in the beginning only a few people chattered confusedly that the souls of the dead slept, and did not really give us to understand what they meant by this statement. Since, however, there have appeared veritable murderers of souls who slaughter them completely without any sign of a wound. . . .'[1]

What is the doctrine that Calvin combats? It is the affirmation that the soul either sleeps after death until the day of judgment, or else that it is a vital breath which, as it is unable to persist without a body, dies with the body until the resurrection of the whole man. Calvin begins by refuting these two opinions by means of a thorough biblical study. Thus from the first he uses the biblical method which will always be his method. In Holy Scripture the soul is not synonymous with life, for there are passages in which the two terms are employed conjointly and in others one term cannot be used in place of the other. For example, 'the multitude of those who believed were of one heart and one soul' (Acts iv. 32) or 'my soul praise the Lord'. The image of God in man cannot be understood of the body, therefore it is situated in the soul. Calvin affirms the immortality of the soul. Jesus exhorted His own people not to fear those who could kill the body, but could not kill the soul (Mt. x. 28). Thus the soul remains after death. The story of the rich man and Lazarus makes it clear that there is a survival of the soul, either in the bosom of Abraham which

[1] Calvin: *Opuscules*, p. 1. Cf. Jacob: *Oeuvres françaises de Calvin* (Paris, 1842), p. 25.

is rest, or in torment. This treatise is a biblical study
which thus inaugurates a new theological method. Calvin
might be reproached for not having shown the distinction
between the soul and the spirit which seems to us to be
clearly taught by holy Scripture (1 Thes. v. 23; Heb. iv.
12) and allows us to solve many of the problems posed by
biblical anthropology.

Towards the end of this year, 1534, Calvin and his
friend, Louis Du Tillet, feeling that their stay in France
was becoming rather precarious, made their way to
Basle via Strasbourg. During the journey, near Metz, one
of their servants stole from them their little leather bag
which contained their money and left them without any
resources. They were able, however, thanks to the money
of another servant, to continue on their way towards
Basle.

Students travelled considerably in the sixteenth century.
In this year, 1534, Angoulême, Nérac, Noyon, Poitiers,
Orleans and Basle were the stops on the way for this
young theologian, greedy for teaching from men and books
alike, eager to bring together the basic principles of the
work he intended to write.

CHAPTER VI

THE INSTITUTES OF THE CHRISTIAN RELIGION

AT Basle Calvin took lodgings at the house of Catherine Klein under the pseudonym of Lucanius, an anagram of his real name. According to Ranner, thirty years afterwards she could recall the austerity and the charm of her lodger. In the town he doubtless discovered his old friend Cop who had taken refuge there, and also Viret and Bullinger. But during this time of study, withdrawn from the world, he was especially occupied with the writing of the *Institution de la Religion chrétienne*.

He must have sketched it in outline at Angoulême. But a sad event was to hasten its publication. During the night of October 17, 1534, theses in the form of placards against the mass were stuck up in several places in Paris and even on the door of the king's room at the Château d'Amboise. Their author was Antoine Marcourt, a native of Lyons, pastor at Neuchâtel and they came from the press of Pierre de Wingle at Serrières. They were aimed at the abuses of the mass and were entitled: *True articles on the horrible, great and unbearable abuses of the papal mass, invented directly against the holy Supper of our Lord, the only Mediator and the only Saviour, Jesus Christ.*[1] Strong words were used: 'I call heaven and earth to witness in truth against this

[1] The text of the placards has been published in Crespin: *Histoire des Martyrs*, Toulouse, 1885, I, pp. 298–302. A facsimile is given in *Images du Passé protestant*, Paris, 1955, p. 37.

pompous and proud papal mass through which the world (if God brings no cure) is and will be totally wasted, wrecked, ruined and lost when our Lord is so outrageously blasphemed in it and the people seduced and blinded; which thing must not be suffered or endured. But in order that the case may more easily be heard by everyone, it is fitting that we should proceed by articles.' In the third of these articles we read, 'Who then can bear it any longer, who can endure such mockery, such pestilential and perverse antichrists—men who, presumptuous and arrogant as they are, according to their usual custom have been so bold and daring as to reach an opposite conclusion [from that of Scripture]? This is why, as enemies of God and His holy Word, they must rightly be exceedingly detested. For, having no shame at wishing to enclose the body of Jesus in their wafer, so, like the brazen heretics that they are, they have had no shame or repugnance at saying that He may be eaten by rats, spiders and vermin, as is written in red letters in the Missals, under the twenty-second canonical precaution. . . . O earth, why do you not open and swallow up these horrible blasphemers? O foul and despicable wretches, is this the body of the Lord Jesus, the Son of God? Does he allow Himself to be eaten by mice and spiders, He who is the bread of angels and of all the children of God? Is He given to us to make of Him food for animals, He who is incorruptible at the right hand of God? Will you make Him subject to worms and rot, against what David has written of Him prophesying His resurrection? O miserable men, if there were no other evil in the whole of your hellish theology except that you speak so irreverently of the precious body of Jesus, how much do you deserve faggots and fire, you blasphemers and heretics—nay, the greatest and most enormous heretics the world has ever seen?

Light your faggots to burn and roast yourselves, then, not us, for we do not wish to believe in your idols, your new gods and your new christs, who can be eaten by animals and by you in the same way, you who are worse than beasts in your triflings over your god of dough, with whom you play like a cat plays with a mouse, pretending to be affected with pity, beating your breasts, after having cut him in three, as if you were very sorry, calling him lamb of God and asking him for peace. St. John pointed to Jesus Christ present, living and entire, who was the truth pre-figured in the Old Testament by the sacrificial lambs. And you show your wafer divided in pieces; then you eat it, and then you have something to drink. Did St. John eat Jesus Christ after this fashion? What would a person be able to say who had never seen such monkey tricks before? Would he not rightly say: "This poor lamb is very far from becoming a sheep, for the wolf has eaten it. . . ." '

The style was violent, the abuse biting. Francis I was extremely angry at what he considered high treason. He reacted brutally, first by ordering processions and prayers, 'to beg God that He would correct these scandalous, heretical placards and books which were nailed or stuck up at several cross-roads and other places in the city of Paris', then by undertaking this correction himself by means of persecution. Calvin was later to write: 'On the occasion of the placards, fury flared up so greatly against the faithful that our cause was made odious.'

Several Evangelicals were arrested and condemned to the stake. The first was the paralytic Barthélemy Milon. Others followed, like Etienne de La Forge, a merchant, who had received and welcomed Calvin in his Paris house.[1]

---

[1] Calvin: *Treatise against the Sect of the Libertines*, ch. IV (*Op. Calv.*, VII, p. 160). Cf. Herminjard: *Correspondance des Réformateurs*, III, p. 166.

Here is what Calvin later wrote about it[1]: 'Whilst I was staying at Basle, being there hidden, as it were, and known by few people, several faithful and holy persons were burned in France. News of this having come to foreign nations, these burnings were greatly deplored by a large proportion of the Germans, and to such an extent that they conceived resentment against the instigators of such tyranny. To smooth the matter over certain wretched little books full of lies were circulated alleging that this cruel treatment was dealt out only to Anabaptists and seditious people who by their vain dreamings and false opinions would overthrow not only religion but all political order.'

In fact Francis I set much store by the alliance of German princes which had been gained by the Reformation. He replied to the accusations which were spread against him by a 'placard' addressed to the Imperial Diet on February 1, 1535.[2] In this he made out that if men had been persecuted for a 'crime of religion' it was because they were raving lunatics urged on by the father of lies. So that if there existed such people amongst the subjects of these princes, they themselves would also have abominated them and considered them accursed. He accused these people of having wished to foment sedition. In short he grouped them with the Anabaptists whose excesses were notorious. The author of this lying controversial pamphlet was, according to Bullinger, Guillaume du Bellay who, at the same instant, was trying to organize conversations between Francis I and certain theologians from Zurich and Germany, particularly Melanchthon. This was a strange double game on the part of these political schemers. In order to flatter the German princes

[1] *Preface to the Commentary on the Psalms (Op. Calv.*, XXI, p. 24).
[2] The text is given in Herminjard: *Op. cit.*, III, p. 249.

and to have them as allies against Charles V they made themselves out to be favourable to the Reformation; yet at the same time they were setting up stakes for the Evangelicals of France.

Calvin goes on: 'Then for my part, seeing that these false plotters by their subterfuges were trying to effect not only the burial of this infamous shedding of innocent blood in unfounded censures and calumnies heaped upon the holy martyrs after their death, but also later were seeking the means to proceed to the last extremity of killing the poor faithful without anyone being able to take pity on them, it seemed to me that unless I were strongly opposed to this, as far as in me lay, I could not exonerate myself from the charge of disloyalty if I remained silent.

'And this was the reason which spurred me on to publish my *Institutes of the Christian Religion*. Firstly, in order to reply to these evil charges which others were sowing and to clear my brothers, whose death was precious before the Lord. Then afterwards, in so far as the same cruelties might soon be practised against many other poor people, so that foreign nations should be at least touched with some compassion and care for them. For I did not produce the book as it is now [1557], a thorough treatment and the result of great toil. It was then only a little booklet containing in summary the principal matters, and it had no other object but that people should be informed what faith was held by those whom I could see evil and lawless flatterers were vilifying in a foul and most mischievous way.'

Such, then, was what might be called the external cause of the publication of the *Institutes* in its first Latin edition—to make known the true doctrine of the persecuted Evangelicals unjustly accused of sedition. Yet we

CHRISTIA

NAE RELIGIONIS INSTI-
tutio,totam ferè pietatis summã,& quic
quid est in doctrina salutis cognitu ne-
cessarium, complectens : omnibus pietatis studiosis lectu dignissi-
mum opus, ac re
cens edi-
tum. ——

PRAEFATIO AD CHRI
stianißimum REGEM FRANCIAE, qua
hic ei liber pro confeßione fidei
offertur.

IOANNE CALVINO
Noxiodunensi autore,

BASILEAE,
M. D. XXXVI.

D. Matthæo Limpærgio sumo
amore Ioan. Oporinus
D. D.

Title page of the first edition of the *Institutes*

must also bear in mind that quite a time before the affair of the placards Calvin had intended to write an exposition of doctrine, a summary of the faith, and that ceaselessly in the course of the different editions he added to his first text, so that the short *enchiridion* of six chapters of 1536 became the dogmatic text book in four volumes and twenty-eight chapters of the years 1559–60.[1]

The booklet of 1536 came from the press of Balthazar Lasius and of Thomas Platter at Basle at the sign of the helmeted Minerva. It is a little volume of 519 pages, easily slipped beneath the cloak. Bertschi writing to Vadianus was to call it a 'catechism of a certain Frenchman'.[2] The Preface, which is addressed 'To the most Christian King of France, Francis the First of this name, his Prince and sovereign Lord', expresses in exalted language the author's aim: 'to serve our French people of whom I can see many who are hungry and thirsty for Jesus Christ and few who have gained a right knowledge of Him.' This letter is dated Basle, 1535, whilst the book itself came from the press only in March, 1536. It was not the first theological work dedicated to Francis I. On December 1, 1523, Erasmus had dedicated to him his *Paraphrase of the Gospel of St. Mark*, edited at Basle. In March, 1525, Zwingli dedicated to him his *True and False Religion* and in 1531 his *Exposition of the Christian Faith* produced at the request of Maigret, French ambassador to the Swiss. But the king accepted these works without reading them, motivated by political reasons only and to give some pleasure to the princes in other countries whom he wished to raise against his enemy, Charles V. The Reformers were not deceived. Bullinger wrote to

---

[1] See the preface to the edition published by the Société Calviniste de France, Labor et Fides, Geneva, 1955.

[2] Herminjard: *Correspondance*, IV, p. 23n.

Bucer: 'I do not know what good we can expect from the king of France; he is a godless and ambitious debauchee.'[1] Doubtless the king never read the epistle that Calvin addressed to him.

The book proper took the form of a relatively undeveloped catechism in this first Latin edition of 1536. The influence of Luther is noteworthy. The plan was that of the German Reformer's *Little Catechism*. Here are the titles of the six chapters which make up the work:

(1) Concerning the law, which contains the explanation of the Decalogue. (2) Concerning faith, in which the Creed called the Apostles' is explained. (3) On prayer, in which the Lord's Prayer is commented upon. (4) Concerning the sacraments, in which Baptism and the Lord's Supper are dealt with. (5) Of the five other sacraments which are not really sacraments although they have hitherto commonly been considered such, and what they are. (6) Concerning Christian liberty, of the power of the Church and the civil government.

This plan was to remain in the catechism that Calvin published in 1537, and of which we shall speak later, and also on a larger scale in the Latin edition of the *Institutes* of 1539 and the French edition of 1541 with their seventeen chapters. But the catechism of 1542, sometimes known as the *Geneva Catechism*, gave up this plan and dealt first with faith, then with the law, then with prayer and finally with the sacraments, under the influence of Bucer, in my opinion. And the final plan of the *Institutes* is quite different.

In 1539 Calvin also produced two prefaces to the Bible which Pierre-Robert Olivétan published the same year under the careful superintendence of the printer Pierre

---

[1] Quoted by J. Pannier: *Epître au Roi de Jean Calvin*, Paris, 1937, p. viii.

de Wingle at Serrières near Neuchâtel. The story of this Bible is well known; it was published as a result of the decision of the assembly of the Waldenses at Chanforans and thanks to the five hundred golden crowns which these poor mountain folk subscribed. Calvin drew up for this Bible a Latin preface dedicated: 'To all emperors, kings, princes and peoples under the rule of Christ.' Departing from the usual custom of publishing a book by the privilege of a prince, Calvin declared that the only privilege which the Bible may claim is that of being the eternal truth of the King of kings, Lord of heaven and earth. Everything about the Reformer bears the stamp of greatness. 'All that I ask,' he said later on, 'is that believing people shall be allowed to hear God speaking to them and to be taught by Him.' The title page of the New Testament in the Bible thus prefaced is headed by the verse John vi. 45 in Greek, 'They shall all be taught of God'. And he goes on, 'When we see men of all states and conditions profiting in the school of God we recognize the truth of the promise of God: "I will pour out my spirit upon all flesh." Certain men rise against this, shuddering with indignation. What is this but reproaching God for His generosity? Ah, if they had lived in the time in which four daughters prophesied in Philip's house, they would have had little patience with them!'

In conclusion, Calvin says, speaking of Olivétan: 'Of the translator I will say only a few words for fear of seeming to ascribe too much to our family ties or to our old friendship. I will say, however, and I believe I can affirm this without fear of denial, that this man is not of slow mind or devoid of scholarship, that he has spared neither work nor research nor toil, and that he has acquitted himself well of his duty as translator. However, there are, I have no doubt, passages which will not please everyone because of the diversity of our apprehension or because in a work of such a length we sometimes fall asleep. I invite the readers if they meet with passages of this nature not to bite a man who is a worthy servant of the sacred Word, not to attack him, but rather to inform him of his lapses in moderate language. This simplicity is suited both to Christian piety and to a doctrine of liberty. We owe no little gratitude to our Robert [Olivétan], who amongst his many gifts possesses that of modesty, and so real a modesty, such excessive humility, that it very nearly prevented his undertaking this holy task, had he not been conquered by the exhortations and even the supplications of these holy men and bold witnesses for the Word, Cusemeth [Farel] and Chlorotes [Viret].'[1]

The second preface, often reproduced in sixteenth- and seventeenth-century Bibles, is frequently given the title, *Epistle to the faithful showing that Christ is the end of the Law.* It is much longer than the first preface and constitutes a veritable treatise on the unity of the two Testaments in Christ. Here is its conclusion as found in the Bible of 1535:

'All good which could be thought or desired is to be found in Jesus Christ alone. For He was humbled to exalt us, He became a slave to free us, He became poor to enrich us, He was sold to redeem us, made captive for our deliverance, condemned for our absolution; He was made a curse for our blessing, an offering for sin for our righteousness, He was marred that we might be restored, He died for our life. So that by Him harshness is softened, anger appeased, darkness made light, injustice justified, weakness made strong, dejection consoled, sin prevented, scorn despised, fear made sure, debt cancelled, toil made light, sadness rejoiced, misfortune made blessed, difficulty eased,

---

[1] We have followed fairly closely the translation of Read in *B.H.P.F.*, 1853, p. 77.

disorder ordered, division united, ignominy made noble, rebellion quelled, threats threatened, ambushes uncovered, assaults assailed, effort weakened, combat combatted, war warred against, vengeance avenged, torment tormented, damnation damned, ruin ruined, hell held prisoner, death done to death and immortality made immortal. . . .'[1]

Here we have the jingling chain of words typical of the language of the sixteenth century, the long enumerations in the fashion of Rabelais, picturesque expressions which distinguish the style of the age.

Towards the end of March, 1536, at the time when the *Institutes* appeared, Calvin left Basle and went with his friend, Louis Du Tillet, to Italy, to the court of Renée of Ferrara. This stay was doubtless only a short one.

Renée of France, daughter of Louis XII and Anne of Brittany, was born at Blois in 1510. If, by the Salic Law, women had not been excluded from the throne of France, Renée would have been queen, being the daughter of the French royal family. But the crown passed to the line of Valois-Angoulême and Francis I became king. He married Renée's sister, Claude. Marriage with Renée was an attractive proposition, and she was in turn engaged to the future Charles V, then later to Henry VIII, king of England, then to the son of the Elector of Brandenburg. In 1527 she married Hercule d'Este, Duke of Ferrara, the son of Lucretia Borgia. She came to Ferrara in 1528. She was intelligent and good-natured, slightly deformed. On intimate terms with her cousin, Marguerite de Navarre, she was very much of the same mind and had perhaps taken the side of the Evangelicals more obviously than Marguerite. She welcomed Clément Marot to her court in 1535. One of her companions was Anne de Parthenay,

[1] *Op. Calv.*, IX, p. 812.

wife of Antoine de Pons, the Count of Marennes, Baron of Oléron, both of whom had been won for the cause of the Reformation. Madame de Pons made known to Calvin the desire that the Duchess had of meeting him and entertaining him at her court for some time. One may imagine the friendly and cultured life of this little Italian town, the pleasant conversation of this cultivated princess, so well-read in ancient literature, and the discussions with the poets and the theologians. What Nérac and the court of Marguerite de Navarre were in France, Ferrara was in Italy around Renée de France.

Under the pseudonym of Charles d'Espeville, Calvin, accompanied by his friend Du Tillet, stayed with the Duchess who welcomed persecuted exiles. To her husband's reproaches she would reply, 'What do you expect me to do? They are poor French folk of my own nation, who would now be my subjects if God had given me a beard on my chin and I had been a man.' It seems that Calvin's stay was, however, of short duration. In the spring of 1536 persecution fell on Clément Marot and other Evangelicals at Ferrara. Calvin did not feel himself secure and had no wish to linger. He had however several conversations with Renée. A letter written by the Reformer later, doubtless in 1537, contained these words to the Duchess: 'I recognized in you such fear of God and such a faithful desire to obey Him that even apart from the lofty station which He has given you amongst men I have a high regard for the graces that He has placed in you, so that I should think myself accursed if I missed occasion to serve you. This I say without any flattery or pretence but in sincerity of heart and speaking as before Him to whom all our secret thoughts are open.' The terms of this letter denote clearly that Calvin had been able to discern the depths of true piety in the one to whom he wrote.

One page in this letter deserves to be quoted in full. It concerns the fight against the mass, the elaboration of which Renée's chaplain, François Richardot, wished more or less to keep going, although he declared himself favourable to evangelical ideas. This facing both ways, rather like that of Gérard Roussel or those who would later be called Nicodemites, gives Calvin the opportunity to inveigh against those who 'under the shadow of the gospel kotow to princes and keep them always by subtleties and cunning wiles in a cloudy haze without leading them straight to their goal.' Here are his own words on this matter:

'In so far as the mass is a sacrifice ordained by men for the redemption and salvation of the living and the dead, as their canon states, it is an intolerable blasphemy in which the sufferings of Jesus Christ are overthrown as if they were of no avail. For what we assert—that the faithful [believers] have been redeemed by the blood of Jesus and have obtained through Him the remission of their sins, righteousness and the hope of eternal life—that must be understood in so far as this loving Saviour, by offering Himself to the Father and by giving Himself up to be killed, offered Himself as an eternal sacrifice through which our iniquities have been purged and cleansed and we ourselves received into the grace of the Father and become partakers of the heavenly inheritance, as the apostle unfolds at sufficient length in the Epistle to the Hebrews. If, therefore, the death of Jesus is not recognized as a unique sacrifice made once and for all in order that it might possess an eternal virtue, what remains for the sacrifice but to be wiped out as if it were of no avail?

'I know quite well that, to cover their abomination, these liars say that they perform the same sacrifice that Jesus made. But thence arise several blasphemies. For this sacrifice could be made only by Himself, and the apostle says that if He is now being sacrificed, He must now still be suffering. Consequently, you can see that one or the other must be true: either we must recognize the horrible blasphemy of the mass and detest it, or by approving it we must trample under foot the cross of Jesus. How different and opposed this is to the Supper of Christ I leave you to consider for yourself after having read in the holy Scriptures of the institution of this Supper. But the great abomination which is committed is the idolatry that is made in it, a creature being adored in the place of God, which is quite inexcusable.'[1]

It was doubtless during his stay at Ferrara that Calvin, if we may believe Colladon, wrote two letters which were not published until 1537. The first of these is entitled *How we must avoid and flee papal superstitions and concerning the pure following of the Christian religion;* the second, *What is the duty of the Christian man in administering or rejecting the benefices of the papal church.*[2] The first was addressed to 'N., a man of upright character, a very special friend.' It is agreed that this man is Nicolas Duchemin of Orleans, who was during his student years one of Calvin's closest friends. Here is how it begins:

'Dearest brother, I am communicating with you but with deepest regret and, as I have to do so, I have compassion and pity on your state and condition, seeing that it is still not lawful for you to extricate yourself and retire out of this Egypt, this place where there are so many proofs of idols and idolatry ever before you and constantly present before your very eyes. Since good men are so

---

[1] *Op. Calv.*, XI, p. 327; J. Bonnet: *Lettres françaises de Calvin*, I, pp. 49, 50.

[2] *Op. Calv.*, V, pp. 233–312 (in Latin); *Opuscules*, pp. 57–131 (in French).

affrighted to hear the rumours and the reports of these things, seeing that the matter is of present concern, sensitive and easily moved folk are of necessity greatly offended, indeed more deeply than can be expressed. You are forced to behold, as you say, evil and impious living amongst monks and priests; and amid the people a thousand kinds of superstition and many a mockery of true religion; everywhere such things abound, one hears and sees nothing else. Those who draw back and turn their eyes away from such a vain display I consider blessed in comparison with your truly wretched obligation, as you depict it. And chiefly, above all other things, the mass (which is the principal source and origin of all abominations) is declared and displayed in the sight of all, and it over-tops and exceeds all other forms of iniquity and wickedness, in which all imaginable or conceivable impiety and iniquity is perpetrated.

'If such sights were only mere games and diversions you would perhaps be able to have a good laugh; but now, as they are serious matters, and great contumely, insult and scorn of God is involved, I have no doubt, as you are a God-fearing man, that they move you rather to anger than to laughter, nay, rather even to tears. Now as for your asking me for advice and discussion as to how you might keep yourself pure and entire for the Lord, unsullied in His service, amid such detestable sacrilege, the pollution and the filth of Babylon in which you have to live for the present according to the condition of the time and your business—this indeed gives me great joy and right willingly will I counsel you and explain how I see the whole matter. And so much the more promptly in that I see many today who, though they wish to be seen as having tasted the things of God, yet do not live lives corresponding to their profession. Chiefly in this matter I see many, nay, very nearly everyone, straying from the true road, and it is not too difficult a matter to advise on this point if you give yourself over entirely to God's discipline and if you allow all your affections to be tamed by His Word.'

The letter continues by showing how the break must be made in a spirit of courage and renunciation. 'Firstly, we must always watch for this and keep our eyes fixed on it: Jesus Christ lays down the law for all His disciples when first He receives them as apprentices in His school. For after He has taught them to begin by denying themselves and carrying their cross, He adds: "Whosoever shall be ashamed of Me and of My words the Son of man will be ashamed of him when He comes in the glory of His Father and with His holy angels." '

We think of the wrench which this stand must have meant in the early days of the Reformation in France. There was not then, as there is today, an evangelical Church, set up with its worship and its doctrine, an already established community ready to receive the believer. By making this break he would enter a solitude caused by separation from his family and all the religious traditions of his youth. He would also enter on a life lived under the constant threat of persecution, the stake, suffering and death. We must not be too severe in our judgment of those who hesitated on the threshold of this break.

After a few weeks Calvin and Du Tillet set out again from Ferrara in the direction of Basle. From there, whilst Du Tillet went to Geneva, Calvin moved to Paris for a short stay in order to set his business in order before settling with his brother and his sister outside France in a town where he would be able to pursue his theological work as he could at Basle. He sold his estate at Noyon and set off towards Strasbourg. The break with his native country had been completed. He was leaving France never to return.

But as the road to the eastern states was barred by warfare the traveller was obliged to make a détour and to enter Switzerland via Lyons and Geneva. Here we must hand over to Calvin, for he himself describes in the preface to the *Commentary on the Psalms* (1557) the way in which he was stopped at Geneva, a place he had intended simply to pass through.

'Master Guillaume Farel held me back in Geneva, not so much by his advice and urgent exhortation as by a fearsome adjuration, as if God from on high had stretched out His hand upon me to stay me. As the most direct road to Strasbourg, whither I wished at that time to retire, was closed by warfare I had decided to slip through Geneva without stopping more than one night in the town. Now a short time previously, popery had been thrown out through the instrumentality of this good person above mentioned [Farel] and by Pierre Viret. But things had not yet settled, and there were divisions and evil and dangerous factions amongst the townsfolk. Then a certain person (who has now most evilly revolted and returned to the papists[1]) discovered me and told others of my presence. Whereupon Farel, who was burning with a better zeal for the advance of the gospel, straightway made every effort to hold me back. Now after he heard that I had some particular study for which I wished to keep myself free, when he saw that he could get nowhere by prayer he even went as far as a curse, that it might please God to curse my rest and the tranquillity for study that I was seeking if in so great a necessity I were to withdraw and refuse

---

[1] Doubtless Du Tillet, who, though a close friend of Calvin, was not to follow him in breaking with Roman Catholicism, and left him in 1538.

to give my help and assistance. This word frightened me and shattered me so much that I set aside the journey I had planned, yet I remained in my shame and timidity, unwilling to have to take on any definite responsibility.'[1]

'As if God from on high had stretched out His hand to stay me!' All Calvin is in this word. Here is the man whom God mastered and tamed, whom He led as by a bridle. Like the apostle Paul he was not disobedient to the heavenly vision. In Farel's voice of thunder, in his curses, in his terrifying adjurations, he hears the very command of God. He does not belong to himself; he obeys. And thus began the unremitting toil which was to forge an indissoluble bond across the pages of history between the name of Geneva and the name of Calvin.

[1] *Op. Calv.*, XXXI, p. 26.

CHAPTER VII

CALVIN'S FIRST STAY AT GENEVA

W HO then was this master Guillaume Farel who in the month of July, 1536, in a room at the Bear Inn had constrained Calvin to stop in Geneva? A few lines will suffice to sketch the main outlines of this character, powerful in word, bold in action, the enthusiastic pioneer of the Reformation.[1]

Born in 1489 at Gap in Dauphiné, Farel came to Paris in 1509, the year Calvin was born, and was therefore his senior by twenty years. He was to study there for twelve years, first as a pupil and then as a teacher in the college of Cardinal Le Moine. It would be quite wrong to consider him as an uncultured man. He quickly became a member of a little group of humanists who were attracted together around Lefèvre d'Etaples in the abbey of Saint-Germain-des-Prés, Gérard Roussel, Michel d'Arande, Guillaume Budé. But, in contrast to these latter, Farel was to break with Rome. He tells us of his conversion in terms similar to those that Calvin was to use: 'I was so soiled with mire and papal filth,' he says in the *True Face of the Cross*, 'and so deeply ruined in it that all that is in heaven and on earth could not have dragged me from it if this loving God and this kindly Saviour Jesus Christ, in His great grace, had not pulled me out by drawing me to His

---

[1] Cf. *Guillaume Farel (1489–1565), Biographie nouvelle* (Neuchâtel and Paris, 1930). This book, written by a group of historians, forms a truly exhaustive biography of the Reformer.

gospel.' And elsewhere, 'But when God, this most kindly Father, taking pity on me in my error, made Himself known to me through a pious brother [Lefèvre] as the God who will be loved and venerated alone, the only one who can save and bless, the only one who can wipe away sin through Christ, the mediator and advocate, the propitiator of sins because He purifies all things by His blood, then my mind was led to Him by various circumstances and having come into port was fixed on Him alone. From then on all things took on a new aspect. Scripture became better understood, the prophets more clear, the apostles more comprehensible, the voice of Christ was recognized as that of the Shepherd, the Master and the Guide.'[1]

After this clear decision, which is generally dated round about 1521, Farel entered into his life of toil for the Reformation, first at Meaux with Briçonnet, then more openly at Gap, his native district. There he met with great difficulties. He was obliged to flee and went to Basle, then to Montbéliard where he openly preached the new gospel in 1524. We find him next as tutor at Aigle in Switzerland (1526), then at Lausanne, at La Neuveville, at Neuchâtel (1531). Urged on by his thunderous voice, which could prevail even over an organ, the people of Neuchâtel invaded the Collégiale, overturned the statues of the saints and went and threw them in the river. Everywhere he went Farel provoked riots but never feared violence. In 1532 we find him in Geneva where his preaching roused the crowd. Accompanied by Olivétan, the future translator of the Bible, and Antoine Saunier, he wished to make the gospel known. But the canons beat him and incited the people to throw him in the Rhone. A blunderbuss shot aimed at him failed to go off. He had to leave the town

[1] These extracts are quoted in *Guillaume Farel*, pp. 105, 106.

with his friends and reached Lausanne. But his attempt at proclaiming the Reformation at Geneva was taken up by Froment, his fellow countryman from Dauphiné, who, in 1533, dared to preach an open-air sermon in the Place du Molard standing on the auctioneer's stone in the fish-market, which must have resembled those still shown at Bourges and Montbéliard as the first evangelical pulpits. After this first public act, and not without many struggles, Protestantism had obtained a footing at Geneva, partly as a result of pressure from Berne. Farel came back to the town at the end of 1533 accompanied this time by Pierre Viret. In March, 1534, swept on by the crowd, he took possession of the Franciscan monastery of Rive and preached there. The Lord's Supper was celebrated there. In 1535, an attempt at poisoning the preachers of the gospel failed, but not without serious effects on Pierre Viret. Tension grew. From May 30 to June 24 a dispute, during discussion of the Rive affair, set the Reformation theologians and those of Rome by the ears. The latter party were finally confounded. Then in May, 1536, the city councillors and the people solemnly proclaimed their resolution to live according to the gospel. However, recalling his arrival in 1536, Calvin could say 'everything was in confusion'.[1] It was Farel's greatness to realize that this tumult must be left behind and that he himself in all the power and fiery vigour of his preaching was not able to give to the nascent church of Geneva the organization and the theological foundation that it needed. It was his greatness too, to be able to efface himself before the young author of the *Institutes*.

Calvin made a humble beginning. He started by preaching a few sermons and his title was simply 'lecturer in holy Scripture' even in 1537. In the register of the council's

[1] *Adieux de Calvin aux Ministres de Genève; Op. Calv.*, IX, p. 892.

78

GENESVE   VILLE ANCIENNE ET RENOMMEE, FIGVREE EN SA PARTIE MERIDIONAL

View of the city of Geneva

decisions, when called upon to refer to some financial subsidy for the newcomer, the secretary, not being able to recall the name, simply wrote: 'that Frenchman' (*ille gallus*). He could not suspect that later this unknown man would become so well known in that same register.

In the later months of 1536 Calvin appears beside Farel as something like a theological counsellor, to whose learning it was at times necessary to refer. At the beginning of October, 1536, a dispute took place at Lausanne between Reformed and Catholic theologians. Berne had just conquered Vaud, and 'their Excellencies' intended forcibly to establish their religion in accordance with the prevailing principle of the sixteenth century in these matters (particularly since the peace of Augsburg in 1555), a principle summed up in the phrase *Cujus regio, hujus religio* (the religion of a country is that of the one who exercises authority in it, that is, the prince or the council). Viret, who had been preaching for several months at Lausanne, and Farel, who had drawn up the theses for the dispute, held leading positions in this public controversy, in which the Catholic position was represented, not by clerics but by laymen, the doctor Blancherose and the captain Ferrand de Loys. At one time, however, Calvin spoke and astounded his audience by the abundance of his quotations from the Fathers and the extent of his patristic learning, in particular on the question of the Lord's Supper.[1]

But his most important work at Geneva was the drawing up of the articles which formed, as it were, the constitution of the church in Geneva, which had until then been 'in tumult'. They were presented on January 16, 1537, by 'master Guillaume Farel and the other

[1] *Op. Calv.*, IX, pp. 877–884.

preachers', but Calvin's style can be recognized in them.[1]

The question which is broached immediately is that of the Lord's Supper. 'It is certain that a church cannot be called well ordered and ruled unless it is one in which the Lord's Supper is often celebrated and frequented, and in such good order that no-one dares to presume to present himself at it unless he comes with especial reverence and in holy fear. And for this reason, in order to keep the church in its integrity, the discipline of excommunication is needful, by which those who are not willing to be docile in full obedience to God's holy Word may be corrected.'

We must not be surprised at the importance which the Reformer attaches to the Lord's Supper. By a strange deviation modern Protestantism has neglected the sacrament and knows little more than the preaching of the Word. The first Reformers, on the contrary, gave to the sacrament of communion with Christ a very large place. They were leaving a church in which the mass was celebrated daily. There were errors in doctrine and practice which had corrupted the sacrament, but these, however, could not lead those who had been constrained to break with them to deprive themselves of the blessing offered in this sacrament. It was in connection with the Lord's Supper that the most serious controversies took place, not only between Reformed and Catholic theologians, but also between various groups of the Reformers themselves. This is a proof of the importance that it had in their spiritual life.

In order to grasp why the question of discipline and excommunication had to be faced at the very start, we must particularly remember that the Reformation in Geneva (as indeed in all countries at that time) was set up,

[1] The text will be found in the collection *Calvin Homme d'Eglise*, Labor et Fides, Geneva, 1936, pp. 1–13.

not by the religious conviction of a few believers desirous of conforming their lives to the Word of God, nor by a popular movement, but by the decision of the councillors who governed the town. The people had become attached to the Reformation through the decision of their leaders. They would therefore crowd in to the Lord's Supper as a body, just as formerly they would crowd in to the mass as a body, in order to go through a religious ceremony rather than out of real piety. In this historical context excommunication is a necessity. It guards the holy table from profanation. It keeps notorious sinners away from the table. This would not be understood by men of our age, in which religious life is a matter of the individual's decision and not the decision of the State. Apart from cases of extreme blindness or defiance, the only people who approach the communion table in our age are believers[1]. Excommunication is self-imposed; it may even play too great a part, for scrupulous persons abstain from the Supper who ought, on the contrary, to take part. Hence we cannot judge the Articles of 1537 from our modern standpoint.

In the first Article Calvin was desirous that the celebration of the Supper should take place every Sunday at least, 'seeing the great consolation that the faithful receive from it and the fruit which proceeds from it in every way, both from the promises which are there presented to our faith (for we are truly made partakers of the body and blood of Jesus, of His death, of His life, of His Spirit and of all His riches), and from the exhortations therein made to us, to recognize and magnify in our

[1] *Translator's note*. The reader will appreciate that M. Cadier writes as a Frenchman having in mind the background of a secular State and a climate of opinion which is largely determined by professed atheism. A national Protestant profession, as in Great Britain, brings its own rather different problems.

praise God's wonderful gift of favour towards us, and finally to live in a Christian manner, being joined together in real peace and brotherly unity as members of a single body'. It will be noticed that in this brief summary we find the three graces which are given us in the Supper: participation in the body and blood of Christ, praise to God, which is the primary sense of the word 'eucharist', and the fellowship of believers with each other. 'It was not instituted by Jesus to be a commemoration two or three times a year but as a frequent exercise of our faith and of our charity.' Calvin therefore desired that the Supper should be celebrated every Sunday.[1]

However, by reason of the people's ignorance, this first Article proposed that the Supper should be celebrated each month and by turns in the three places in which, at that time, preaching took place: St. Peter, Rive and St. Gervais. This proposal was not agreed to by the Council, which insisted on a celebration four times a year, at the three great festivals and in September. Calvin accepted the decision with regret. 'I gave in too easily', he was to say later. And unfortunately this Genevan decision was to remain until our day the [French] Protestant custom, contrary to Calvin's deepest conviction.

In order that the Supper should not be profaned by those who were in no way members of the body of Christ, Calvin set up a disciplinary system of reproof and control, and to this end he asked the Council to establish a system of overseers. 'Let it be your pleasure to ordain and elect certain persons of good life and reputation from amongst the body of the faithful who are likewise men of integrity and not easily corrupted, who, being scattered in all quarters of the town, may keep an eye on the life and

[1] See also on this point *Inst.*, IV, xvii, 43 and 44.

conduct of every person[1]; and if they see any notable vices to be admonished in anybody, let them communicate with one of the ministers in order to censure whoever is at fault and to exhort him in a brotherly manner to amend his ways.'

Here, then, we have the institution of the 'overseers' who were to characterize the new organization of the Calvinist Church by the commital of authority to this group of elders (in Greek, *presbuteroi*). This is the 'presbyterian' system, which entrusts to this group, to the *presbytery*, the ruling of the church, instead of entrusting it to a *bishop* (the 'episcopalian' system). But we are merely studying the very beginning here. These elders of the 1537 Articles were nominated by the State and not by the Church. Their responsibility was moral oversight and not the direction of the parish. It would be years before these men were released from the control of the State to give the Church its autonomy. Calvin was not to see the setting up of a true presbyterian system, as he had conceived it, during his lifetime. But it is no less true that the principle had been laid down. On the one hand, a personal confession of faith would be demanded of every member of the Church. 'Let every inhabitant have to make his confession and give a satisfactory account of his faith in order that it may be known which people are in harmony with the gospel and which would prefer to belong to the kingdom of the pope rather than to the kingdom of Jesus Christ.' So much for the composition of the Church. It was for the elders, on the other hand, to watch over the discipline of this Church. So much for its constitution.

---

[1] This is the original meaning of the Greek word *episcopoi*—'those having an eye on', 'overseers'. The word *episcopoi* became our word 'bishop'.

In their second paragraph the Articles deal with the singing of Psalms by the entire congregation. This was a new thing and harked back to the primitive Church. Singing was no longer reserved for cantors or choirs; it became once more the expression of the prayers and praises of church people. 'The psalms will be able to move us to raise our hearts to God and to stir up in us a zeal both to call upon Him and to exalt the glory of His name in praise.'

A third Article spoke of the teaching of children and the necessity of training them by a catechism in order that they might then be able to testify to their faith. Calvin had already prepared this catechism. It was not drawn up in the form of questions and answers. Its title was *Instruction and Confession of Faith used in the Church of Geneva*. At the head of the first page there are three verses from the first Epistle of Peter. 'As newborn children desire the reasonable milk which is without guile' (ii. 2); 'Be ready to give an answer to anyone who asks of you a reason for the hope that is in you' (iii. 15); 'If anyone speaks let him speak as the oracles of God' (iv. 11). This *Instruction* is a summary of the *Institution chrétienne* of 1536. It is therefore the first systematic exposition of Calvinist thought in the French language, far too full, moreover, to be taught to children. It is a textbook of doctrine, not an educational handbook. In his preface to the Latin translation of 1538, Calvin called it 'an authentic public testimony of our doctrine', to make known to the other churches the faith of the church of Geneva and to enable them to unite with her.

To this *Instruction* was joined the 'Confession of Faith which all citizens and inhabitants of Geneva and subjects of the region must swear to hold and to keep, taken from the *Instruction* used in the church of the said town'. It contained twenty-one Articles. By a personal acceptance of this confession of faith one became a member of the church. Those who refused had simply 'to go and live somewhere else'. We may guess at the difficulties that such a demand by the Reformers would produce.

Before we embark on the exposition of these ecclesiastical struggles, however, we must speak of the first conflict that Calvin had at a theological level. This was the controversy with Pierre Caroli. Extraordinary as it may seem, Farel and Calvin were accused of denying the doctrine of the Trinity. In 1531 Servetus had published a little treatise, *De Trinitalis erroribus* ('On the errors of the Trinity'), in which for the first time since the fourth century Trinitarian doctrine was attacked. Now Calvin was accused of being a disciple of Servetus. Caroli, however, the man who had formulated the accusation, well knew the men he was accusing. A native of northern France and a former student at Paris, disciple of Lefèvre d'Etaples and friend of Briçonnet, Caroli had thrown in his lot with the Evangelicals. In 1535 the persecution consequent upon the affair of the placards obliged him to flee to Geneva. There he fell out with Farel and Viret.

In 1536 he was nominated principal pastor of Lausanne by the Bernese. At that point he began to recommend prayers for the dead to his flock. Calvin and Viret reproached him for this return to a Roman doctrine and lodged a complaint with the pastors of Berne. Caroli replied by accusing them of being anti-Trinitarian. Calvin then presented as his defence part of the *Instruction* of 1537 which he had just published. Doubtless he drew attention to these lines from the beginning of the explanation of the Creed: 'In order that our confession of belief in Father, Son and Holy Spirit may perturb nobody, we must first say a little about it. When we speak of the Father, the Son, and the Holy Spirit we do not imagine that there are three gods, but Scripture and godly experience itself show us in the very simple essence of God, the Father, His Son and His Spirit. Thus our mind cannot conceive of the Father without similarly understanding the Son, in whom His express image shines, and the Spirit, in whom all His power and virtue appears. Let us, then, remain with every thought of our heart settled on one God alone, and yet let us contemplate the Father with the Son and His Spirit.'

That ought to have been enough. However, Caroli summoned his interlocutors to declare that they adhered to the three ancient Creeds of the early Church, the Apostles' Creed, the Nicene Creed, and the Athanasian Creed. Calvin refused saying, 'we have sworn faith in one God and not in Athanasius, whose Creed was not approved by any true church.'

This reply has always caused much surprise, for it seemed to offer grounds for Caroli's objections. Calvin, however, was intent upon stressing that his faith was based on the Word of God and on nothing else. To agree to be bound by an ecclesiastical Creed, however venerable it might be, seemed to put the seat of doctrinal authority somewhere other than in Holy Scripture. His reservations concerned essentially the Athanasian Creed, and modern criticism has justified him. It is now recognized that this Creed is falsely attributed to Athanasius and has not the authority the Greek Church and also the Anglican Church have given it. But Calvin was particularly emphatic in his refusal to admit that he could be blamed for having deliberately left out of his catechism of 1537 the terms 'Trinity', 'substance', 'person'—theological terms which did not seem to him in place in a confession of faith based on Holy Scripture. Besides, his *Institution chrétienne* of 1536 contained sufficiently clear statements on this matter. 'We confess that we believe that the Holy Spirit is truly God with the Father and with the Son, third person of the most holy Trinity, consubstantial and co-eternal with the Father and with the Son, all-powerful, creator of all things. There are three distinct persons and one single essence.' Caroli could have consulted this document. What clearer statement could he demand? A synod met at Lausanne on May 14, 1537. Calvin and Farel defended themselves with vigour and Caroli's accusations were dismissed. Shortly afterwards Caroli went back to France, returned to the Roman Church, became a Protestant again in 1539, and returned to Roman Catholicism once more in 1543. The calumnies of this quarrel had, however, not left the reputation of the Genevan Reformers unharmed. Even Melanchthon had realized this. In the harshness with which he was later to deal with the anti-Trinitarian Servetus, Calvin was certainly taking care to demonstrate that the accusations of Caroli were without any foundation.

Let us now return to other difficulties, those which the application of the 1537 Articles met with in Geneva. They were presented to the Little Council on January 16, 1537. On March 13 this Council decided they should be fully observed. On July 29 the Council of the Two Hundred ordered the 'dizeniers', that is leaders of the districts or 'dizaines' of the town, to bring the groups of townsfolk of their jurisdiction to St. Peter's to swear to the confession of faith there. There were some objectors. On November 12 the order to submit or retire was renewed. The tension grew. Calvin might then have contented himself with the results he had gained and moderated his demands, but he was determined to stand firm. At the beginning of January, 1538, the Reformers Farel, Calvin, and Coraud, the blind pastor, warned the Council that they believed they were obliged to exclude from communion those who had not sworn their adherence to the confession of faith. The Council decided that no-one should be refused permission to participate in the Lord's Supper. The question now was to decide to whom belonged spiritual authority and the right of exercising the discipline of the Lord's table—to the pastors or to the town Council, to the spiritual power or to the temporal power.

When seeking to understand the situation of a country in the first half of this sixteenth century, we must never forget the fact that the State, in the form of prince or Council, was totalitarian, that it wished to direct everything, and in particular the life of the Church, and that the Lutheran Reformation, by having recourse to the princes, gave them complete authority in this domain. Now it was Calvin's wish that authority should belong to the pastors as far as the religious life was concerned. And so, when at the beginning of 1538 the Council of the Two Hundred decided that they would live according to God and according to the ceremonies of the Church at Berne, and took to themselves the right to regulate the life of the Church, this seemed to Calvin inadmissible. And we can only congratulate him on having desired the independence of the Church. The Bernese ceremonies, less radical than the Genevan ceremonies, had retained baptismal fonts, unleavened bread in the Lord's Supper and the observation of the great Christian festivals. Granted that these things were of secondary importance; but Berne had a spirit of domination and wished to introduce conformity to its own method of worship into Geneva. On March 11,

1538, the Council of the Two Hundred voted for this conformity. It then asked the pastors to submit. Coraud refused and preached, despite the prohibition of the Council. He was put in prison. Calvin and Farel protested against the imprisonment of their colleague. They were refused the right to preach. On Easter Day, despite the prohibition of the Council, Calvin preached in St. Peter's and Farel at St. Gervais. It was communion day but they refused to hold the communion service, not because they thought the Bernese use of unleavened bread bad in itself, but because they considered that to administer the Lord's Supper at a time of popular disturbance 'would be to profane so holy a mystery'. The Councils met on April 23, and by a majority vote of the General Council, Farel, Calvin and Coraud were ordered to leave Geneva within three days.

'Right! well and good!', exclaimed Calvin when informed of his banishment. 'If we had served men we should have been ill requited. But we serve a great Master, who will reward us.'

CHAPTER VIII

CALVIN AT STRASBOURG

THE day after their banishment Calvin and Farel departed for Basle. While Farel rapidly betook himself to Neuchâtel in the place of Antoine Marcourt, the author of the placards, who had been called to Geneva, Calvin remained some time in this town, the centre of learning where the first edition of the *Institutes* had been published two years previously. Another edition was needed and he intended to work there quietly, taking up his theological researches again. But the Strasbourg Reformers, Bucer, Capito and John Sturm, wrote to him, asking him to come to their town to exercise some small ministry there (*parvum ministeriolum*). Calvin would not comply. Then Bucer, using a warning similar to that of Farel at Geneva, threatened Calvin with the divine wrath and reminded him of the example of Jonah, the rebellious prophet whom God had to pursue even in the storm. 'Terrified by this example', Calvin yielded. So he found himself in Strasbourg despite himself, just as he had done at Geneva, led on by a hand from on high. As soon as he arrived he set to work as preacher to the refugees driven out of France by persecution. On Sunday, September 8, 1538, he preached for the first time in the Church of Saint-Nicolas-aux-Ondes, not far from the ramparts.

Strasbourg was a cross-roads between France, Germany, Switzerland and the Low Countries. Various currents of

Reformation thought met there. German Lutherans stood side by side with French Evangelicals, Anabaptists from the Low Countries and Zwinglians from Switzerland. All the various doctrines mingled in a great stream of life and activity under the peaceable direction of Bucer. For three years Calvin was to be a friend and disciple of Bucer.

The recent work of Strohl and Courvoisier has shown the paramount influence of Bucer over Calvin's development. Seventeen years older than his young colleague, Bucer inspired in him great admiration. Calvin considered him as an elder brother, a master, a man through whom he could reach the first generation of Reformers, a man who had been in direct contact with Luther and who had fought against anabaptism. Though in 1538, what we might call Calvin's systematic theology is already largely fixed by the *Institution chrétienne* and its summary, the Catechism of 1537, his practical theology is still to be made clear, and the painful experiences at Geneva showed him the difficulty of organizing the resurgent Church. Now he was to gain much profit in the school of Bucer.

The most serious question that confronted Calvin was that of the discipline of the Lord's Supper. It was on this point that he had been out-voted at Geneva and had been forced to leave; but he had not on that account in any way given up his conviction that great respect was due to the sacrament. He had indeed the vision of an open Church, uniting the people of the town or the nation in the service of God. But at the same time he wished to safeguard the purity and the sincerity of those who came to the Lord's table. Communion could be taken only by believers, members of the body of Christ, really receiving communion with their Saviour. At Strasbourg Calvin replaced the Roman Catholic confession by a private interview with the pastor. Those who wished to communicate had to come to see him beforehand, 'in order that the ignorant, who had been poorly instructed in religious matters, should be better prepared, in order that those who needed special admonishing should receive it, and in order that those who were troubled by some distress of conscience should be comforted'. He declared that he could not suppress the Roman Catholic confession if it were not replaced by this interview. Here, certainly, was a point on which the Reformation movement as a whole was too drastic. Without restoring the sacrament of penance, it should have upheld more firmly the prior interview with the pastor or the elder.

As far as the discipline of the Supper was concerned, Bucer had realized how necessary this was as early as 1531, and established parochial overseers (the *Kirchen-pfleger*) numbering three for each parish and taken in equal numbers from amongst the members of the town Council, the magistrates and members of the parishes. They were nominated by the government and not by the Church. But Bucer had clearly seen, as Œcolampadius and later Calvin were to see, that it was the Church's duty to nominate these elders. 'God is a God of order', he said; 'that is why St. Paul always set up, or had others set up, a system of elders within the churches . . . who were to maintain sound doctrine intact and to stop the mouths of those who opposed themselves . . . that is the express command of God. It is therefore good, it must continue, and all Christians must conform to it. . . . Everyone must be exhorted rigorously to observe such an ordinance given to us by the Holy Spirit Himself.' And Bucer, clarifying his thoughts later (in 1536) realized that there must not only be one minister of the Word but several ministers in the Church. He was the first to speak of the four ministries, that is, those of pastor, teacher, elder and deacon. Thus

it is from Bucer that Calvin borrowed his famous distinction of the four ministries which is fundamental in
Reformed discipline. When he came back to Geneva in
1541 Calvin was to establish in the Ordinances the four
ministries according to Bucer's theory.

In the domain of liturgy Calvin also borrowed from
Bucer and the Strasbourg liturgy the form of church
prayers. 'As for the Sunday prayers I took the form of
Strasbourg and borrowed the larger part of it.'[1] In
particular, from Strasbourg comes the confession of sins,
which is still in the Sunday morning liturgy. It is a translation of a German text, probably by Bucer, on which
Calvin has left the marks of his style and the elevated tone
of his language. We know what a deep impression this
prayer produced when it was pronounced by Theodore
Beza at the beginning of the Colloquy of Poissy in 1561.
But as early as 1542 Calvin had set it in the Genevan
liturgy. From Bucer also, Calvin borrowed the plan for his
catechism of 1542, so different from the one which he had
published in 1537.

For a comparison of Bucer and Calvin we may borrow
the following passage from Jaques Courvoisier: 'Clearly
we are dealing with men of quite different personality,
stature and character. Calvin is as logical, orderly and
clear as Bucer is unlogical, unclear and involved. When
the former writes a commentary everything is balanced,
everything is in its place and the arrangement of the book
is immediately apparent. Whereas when Bucer writes a
commentary there is no proportion. He will write end-
lessly on passages which are not always worth the trouble,
yet elsewhere he will settle in five lines questions of
greatest importance . . . when you read Calvin after
having waded through Bucer you often have the impres-

[1] Calvin's last words.

sion of a distilled, pruned, clarified Bucer who has succeeded in fully mastering his thoughts.

'Another difference which is obvious on a short acquaintance with Bucer and Calvin is that Calvin has a theological sensitivity which is much keener than that of Bucer. We might compare Bucer with a great, powerful, flowing river whose waters are, however, difficult to canalize. Bucer brings down as many nuggets of gold as he does common pebbles in his work. But the most serious fact is that he generally does not know how to distinguish the gold from the pebbles. The whole thing comes higgledy-piggledy and is borne along by the vigour of an exceptional personality and a mighty intellect. Calvin, for his part, knows how to distinguish the gold from the pebbles, and if it is interesting to note what Calvin borrowed from Bucer, it would be just as significant to notice what he left untouched, for he ignored certain aspects of his work, notably the confirmation of the 'catechumens' and the institution of informal little assemblies within the churches in which people could more freely submit to discipline, assemblies which later inspired Spener and the whole pietist movement of the seventeenth and eighteenth centuries.

'Finally, a feature which distinguishes one Reformer from the other, and which it is no less needful to mention, concerns their character. Bucer is far more irenical than Calvin. Far more than the latter he wishes to maintain peace at any price and that often led him, notably in his dealings with Luther, to certain concessions which give both his theology and his work a certain wavering quality.'[1]

Calvin was not only pastor at Strasbourg, he was also teacher. He gave lessons in the New Testament, in the

[1] J. Courvoisier, 'Bucer et Calvin' in *Calvin à Strasbourg, 1538–1938.*

High School that Jacob Sturm had just founded in 1538 with his namesake John Sturm, who was a magistrate and not a headmaster. He used to teach daily, his salary being a florin per week. His theological works of that period are important. It was at Strasbourg in 1539 that he had printed by Wendelin Ribel the second Latin edition of the *Institution chrétienne*, 'now really corresponding to its title' (*nunc vere demum suo titulo respondens*). In fact the format of the first edition of 1536 was that of a booklet, easily concealed, a volume which could be slipped under the cloak. It contained six chapters. The 1539 edition is a theological book in large format, a desk volume, almost folio size. It has seventeen chapters and the subjects are more fully dealt with. This was the text which was two years later to be translated into French by Calvin himself and to become the first French edition of 1542.

It was at Strasbourg that he published his first commentary, that on the Epistle to the Romans (October 18, 1539), dedicated to Simon Grynée 'a man endowed with excellent graces', one of the professors at Basle who had welcomed him in his house. This commentary shows clearly that Calvin was, from the first, a prince of exegetes, 'studying', he tells us himself, 'to be readable and clear', and an enemy of long-windedness. In his preface he mentions the modern commentaries by Melanchthon, Bullinger and Bucer, and gives to each the praise which it deserves.

At Strasbourg too, he wrote the *Epistle to Sadoletus*.[1] The humanist Jacques Sadolet (1477–1547) was an Italian prelate who had been at the court of Rome and, more particularly, had served as Secretary of Leo X in 1513, and then become the bishop of Carpentras. He had the

[1] Latin text in *Op. Calv.*, V, pp. 369–384; French text in *Opuscules*, pp. 131–174.

reputation of a peace-maker, and his friendship with Erasmus classed him amongst the scholars. Elevated to the rank of cardinal in 1538, he wrote a letter to the people of Geneva inviting them to return to the Church of Rome, stressing the perpetuity of this Church 'approved by unanimous consent for the last fifteen centuries', in the face of 'the novelties introduced in these latter twenty-five years by men who are either over-bold or believe themselves clever'. The Genevans received this letter and transmitted it to the authorities at Berne; the latter asked Calvin to reply to it. Calvin might have objected that Geneva's problems were no concern of his any more, since he had been banished from the town. Besides, had it not been Sadolet's intention to make some sort of capital out of this absence to try to reconquer the Genevans? But Calvin did not dwell on personal questions. The cause of God alone mattered to him. He accepted the invitation to write a reply; it took him only six days and it is a marvel of lively wit and sound exposition. Calvin does not hesitate to strike a personal note occasionally: 'But O Lord thou hast enlightened me by the brightness of thy Spirit . . . thou hast placed before me thy Word as a lamp to show me how pernicious and evil these things are; thou hast touched my heart in order that I should rightly and truly abominate them'. And he addresses his adversary vigorously: 'There is not much of a real theologian about a person who is so keen to force another man into his own straitjacket, while at the same time he never instructs him that the starting-point of a well-directed life is to desire, to increase and to adorn the glory of the Lord, seeing that we are principally born for God and not for ourselves.'

It was at Strasbourg too that Calvin published a collection of Psalms. In the early days Reformed worship was made up of reading, exposition of the Bible and prayers. But following the example of the German Reformation, the French Reformers wished to have singing in their own language. In 1539 appeared the first collection: *Some Psalms and Canticles set to Music*. It contained eighteen Psalms and three canticles, the Nunc Dimittis, the Ten Commandments, and the Creed. (We must not forget that in early Reformed worship the Creed was sung by the whole congregation.) Marot had translated some of the Psalms but there were seven from the hand of Calvin himself. Later Calvin withdrew his translations and replaced them with those by Marot and Beza. There was no author's pride in Calvin. Yet his poetry was not bad. Here is the first verse of the setting of Psalm xlvi:

> *Notre Dieu nous est ferme appui*
> *Auquel aurons en notre ennui*
> *Vertu, forteresse et sûr confort,*
> *Présent refuge et très bon port.*
> *Dont certaine assurance aurons*
> *Même quand la terre verrons*
> *Par tremblement se derrocher*
> *Et monts en la mer se cacher.*

Some years later a Walloon student passing through Strasbourg in 1545 wrote to a friend: 'You would never believe what a happy thing it is and what peace of conscience one experiences in being where the Word of God is purely proclaimed and the sacraments purely administered.[1] Also when one hears the fine Psalms sung and the marvellous works of the Lord. . . . At the beginning when I heard the singing I could scarcely keep myself from weeping with joy. You would not hear one

[1] The Calvinist definition of the Church is recognizable here. See *Inst.*, IV, i, 9.

The Knobloch Press, rue de la Demi-Lune, Strasbourg

voice drowning another. Everybody holds a book of music in his hand. Every man and woman alike praises the Lord.'

It is not hard to imagine that with such pastoral and theological labour Calvin's days were very full. He wrote to Farel on April 20, 1539: 'When the messenger came to take the beginning of my book I had to read twenty pages [i.e. eighty pages of proofs to correct]. Moreover I had a lesson, a sermon and four letters to write, a certain controversy to settle and more than ten visitors I had to reply to.'

Among these labours, we note Calvin's reference to controversy. In particular he had to deal at Strasbourg with the Anabaptists who rejected infant baptism. Towards the end of his life he was to recall his success in these discussions and the large number of children who were brought to him from five or ten leagues around so that he might administer baptism to them. Among the Anabaptists whom he brought back to the Church we must mention John Stordeur, of Liège, who died sometime after of the plague, and whose widow Calvin married.

This brings us to Calvin's marriage. He was not yet thirty and was in no way romantic. His idea of marriage may perhaps seem rather selfish. 'The only beauty that attracts me is this,' he wrote to Farel, 'that she should be modest, obliging, not arrogant, thrifty, patient and careful for my health.' He was to find this unreserved devotion in Stordeur's widow, Idelette de Bure. Their union was happy but was not to last for long, for she died in 1549. We know very little of her. Bucer described her as *brave et honnete*, which means well-dressed in the conventional fashion. Farel says that she was 'upright, decent and fair'. A short time after her death, which was the outcome of a long illness patiently borne, Calvin wrote to Viret: 'I have been deprived of my excellent life-companion who, if it had been necessary, would have faced with me not only exile and poverty, but even death. As long as she lived she was my faithful helper in the ministry. She was never the least hindrance to me.'

'Exile and poverty.' These two words give us an insight as to how hard life was for Calvin and his wife on the material level. Their resources were small and the salary poor. He used to sell his books in order to get money for food. The printer Ribel sometimes made him advance payments. Although he had been received as a citizen of Strasbourg and registered in the guild of tailors (though doubtless he had never held a needle), Calvin felt that he was an exile, far from his country, deprived of his possessions which were still in France. Their only child, Jacques, born on July 28, 1542, lived but a few days. Some years later, in the course of discussions at Geneva, one of his adversaries reproached him coarsely for the fact that he had no children. Calvin then gave this prophetic reply: 'My sons are to be found all over the world'. God who had refused him the joys of physical fatherhood had granted him those abounding joys of spiritual fatherhood.

Towards the end of his stay at Strasbourg Calvin was called to take part in several discussions between the Roman Catholics and the Protestants, in Frankfurt (April 1539), at Haguenau (June, 1540), at Worms (November 1540), at Ratisbon (April 1541). By these discussions the Emperor Charles V wished to obtain a compromise which would have halted the division of Christianity. At Frankfurt, Calvin met Melanchthon whose close friend he became. The learned German theologian, older than Calvin, a man of deep understanding, drawn by his peace-loving temperament towards compromises, could not but feel himself akin to the young Frenchman whose courage and learning he recognized. In 1543 Calvin dedicated to Philip Melanchthon his reply to Pighius, the *Treatise on Free Will*, one of the most important of the Reformer's writings. Unfortunately this work has been left in obscurity too long, not having been re-edited in French since the sixteenth century. In 1546 Calvin published and wrote a preface to the French translation of Melanchthon's classic work, the *Loci communes*. He had the greatest of respect and the deepest admiration for the 'tutor of the Germans'.

Calvin never met Luther. The latter seems to have concerned himself but little with the French Reformer. They were men of a different genius. Their ages separated them and neither understood the other's language, though it is true that through Latin they could meet in their writings. Calvin attached much value to a report of Luther's commendation which the latter communicated to him through Bucer after the reply to Cardinal Sadolet.

In his pamphlet, *Histoire de la Vie, des Ouvrages et des Doctrines de Calvin* (1842), M. Audin recounts a story which is worth mentioning:

'There was at Wittemberg a bookseller named Moritz Goltz, whose shop was frequented by scholars and professors. One day, Doctor Martin had just been lecturing on Genesis and was leaving the college surrounded by a swarm of pupils when he stopped in front of the bookseller's stall: "Well now!" he said to him, "What do they say of me at Frankfurt? Do they still want to burn the great heretic, Martin?"—"No master", replied the bookseller, "but here is a little book which comes from there and which deals with the Lord's Supper. Its author is Master John Calvin, who originally wrote it in French and Nicolas des Gallars has translated it into Latin. They say the author is a young man of great knowledge and piety

and that in this book he shows how you have gone astray
with Zwingli and Œcolampadius, on the article of the
sacrament."—"Really", said Luther laughing, "show it
me then, Moritz, so that I may glance through it." Then
Moritz went and got an octavo volume from the shelves of
his shop which he handed to the Doctor. Luther sat down
and began to read the first pages closely. Then he had a
swift glance over the few chapters and the contents page,
and gave the book back to the bookseller with the words
"He is a man of faith and scholarship. If Œcolampadius
and Zwingli had dealt with the business as he does, the
dispute would have been shorter and less bitter." '

From his side, Calvin wrote to Bullinger on November
25, 1544: 'I learn that Luther with his bold intemperance
assails us all together. I cannot in all honesty hope that
you will remain silent. For, after all, it is not right to be
so ill-treated and never dare to defend oneself. I confess
that Luther is a rare genius who has received extraordinary
treasures from heaven. He possesses a wonderful strength
of soul and a constancy under all trials, having fought
antichrist [the pope] even until this day. I have often said
that, even if he were to treat me as a devil incarnate, I
should none the less consider him a great servant of
Christ.'

In March, 1541 Calvin went to Ratisbon with Bucer.
There they met Melanchthon, who had insisted that
Calvin should be present 'because of his great reputation
among the scholars'. On the Roman Catholic side there
was Eck, Luther's old adversary, and as papal nuncio,
Cardinal Contarini, a moderate. There was also Pighius,
who threatened to attack Calvin with his pen and actually
wrote against him in 1542 his *Treatise on Free Will and
Divine Grace*, dedicated to Cardinal Sadolet. We have

already referred to the answer to this which Calvin published in 1543.

No positive result was to come from these conferences. Calvin made every effort to plead the cause of the French, who were being so cruelly persecuted. He would have liked an alliance to be established between the German princes and Francis I, against the emperor Charles V. Marguerite d'Angoulême, Queen of Navarre, thanked Calvin in a letter on behalf of King Francis I, her brother. Nevertheless, for all that, the position of the king did not change as regards the Evangelicals.

However, for some time the political situation had been different in Geneva. The friends of Guillaume Farel, who for this reason were called 'guillermins', had retained their affection for the two banished Reformers. They would even have liked to abstain from the Lord's table to register their discontent. Calvin dissuaded them from this out of horror of schism. But their influence was on the increase. They had against them those in favour of the alliance with Berne who were called 'artichokes', because of the articles in the Treaty with the Berne authorities which were particularly opposed by the Genevan patriots. The situation was very disturbed. Towards the end of 1540, as soon as the guillermins were in power, they attempted to bring Calvin back, but the latter would not leave Strasbourg at any price to go back to the turbulent city which had thrown him out. 'I should prefer a hundred other deaths rather than this cross on which I should have to die a thousand times a day,' he wrote to Farel. The latter was not discouraged and returned to the charge several times. He even went to Strasbourg to issue a new summons similar to that which he had made to Calvin to keep him in Geneva the first time. Here again Calvin is trembling, afraid to 'throw off the yoke of the calling which he knows God has laid upon him'. Finally he gave in and wrote to Farel on October 24, 1540: 'If I had any choice I would rather do anything than give in to you in this matter, but since I remember that I no longer belong to myself, I offer my heart to God as a sacrifice.'

All Calvin is in this last phrase. The man whom his enemies even today have made out to be a proud man full of dark ambitions, thirsting for power, is on the contrary humble, timid and a man who acts only under the influence of spiritual constraint. His strength is not that of ambition, but rather of obedience, naked obedience to the God whom he recognizes as his Lord. 'I do not belong to myself.' When later, on the threshold of the little treatise on the Christian life which he inserted into the *Institutes* in Book III, chapters vi–x, Calvin was to speak of denying oneself, he could not speak of it coldly or didactically, but with the fervour of personal experience. 'We are not our own, we belong to the Lord. We are not our own. Let our reasons and our wills then never predominate in our thinking and in our acting. . . . We are not our own. Let us then forget ourselves as much as is possible. . . . O how well a man has profited if he has recognized that he is not his own and has taken the lordship and rule of himself away from his own reason and handed it over to God!'

'I offer my heart to God as a sacrifice.' These words from the letter to Farel were to become henceforth Calvin's motto. He pictured them by a hand holding a heart and the Latin words: *Prompte et sincere.*

Yet Calvin's departure from Strasbourg for Geneva was not prompt. He might almost be said to have postponed his return. He was given the opportunity to do this by his taking part in the discussions at Worms and Ratisbon. From the Inn at Ulm he wrote to Farel: 'You have shattered and scared me with the thunderbolts with which you rage in so strange a fashion.' In the end, without any ceremony, he entered Geneva once more on September 13, 1541.

CHAPTER IX

THE PREACHER OF THE WORD OF GOD AT GENEVA

THE following Sunday Calvin went up into the pulpit at Geneva, and simply began again to expound holy Scripture at the place where he had broken off when he had been banished. The brackets were closed. Without recrimination or proclamation, the servant of the Word of God was taking up his responsible task again. He was to be nothing else but the bold and indomitable preacher of this Word.

If he had been hounded out of the town, it was because the magistrates and the town Council had wished to hold the whip-hand in the Church and impose their will upon the pastors. That he was now back was due to the fact that he had obtained freedom to establish a spiritual dominion and he had caused the authority of the pastors to be respected.

Calvin's name is continually coupled with the title 'Dictator'. It is regarded as an established fact, an unqualified description. But can one call a man a dictator who was never in any of the councils of the town, did not receive the citizenship of Geneva until four years before his death, and never had a police force or an army at his disposal? We are then told that it was a spiritual dictatorship, a dogmatic dictatorship. But how can these words be conjoined, and in what sense can a spiritual authority, however great it may be, be called a dictatorship? Granted, Calvin was more or less permanent chairman of the Company of pastors. He was professor of theology; he preached daily and had a vast correspondence with men of several countries; and he had a definite influence on the Consistory of which, however, he was not chairman. But we must repeat: the spiritual authority of an exceptional personality distinguished for his faith, his theological knowledge and his entire consecration to the cause of God, cannot be called a dictatorship, particularly in an age such as ours which knows from sad experience what this word really signifies.

View of the lake from the windows of
Calvin's house

Can one give the name of dictatorship to the activity of a man whose life at Geneva was a struggle to the very end and who, for example, never succeeded in disentangling the life of the Church from the power of the magistrate, and was obliged right to the end to allow the city councillors to preside at the sessions of the Consistory and to nominate the elders? Can one use the term 'dictatorship' to describe the tenacity of a man determined to gain respect for the truth of God and the freedom of the pastors' decisions as to the participation in the Lord's Supper of any particular believer? Our age has witnessed the separation of the two powers, spiritual and temporal, and the thought would never occur to us to maintain that the State should take decisions in the spiritual realm. Hitler found out something about this for himself. Why then should we treat as a dictator a man like Calvin who simply wished to have the primacy of the spiritual realm respected in Geneva?

A month after his arrival in Geneva the ecclesiastical ordinances usually known as those of 1541, which Calvin had drawn up in twenty days, were adopted by the councillors. Under the influence of Bucer and putting into practice what he had learnt from the Strasbourg Reformer, Calvin established at Geneva the 'Four Ministries' which are fundamental to the Calvinist Church: pastors, teachers, elders, and deacons.

The pastors were nominated by their colleagues subject to the approval of the Smaller Council of the town. The people had only the right of common consent which was not very much. Calvin would have liked the induction of the pastor to be by the laying on of hands, that is, a ceremony rather like our present-day 'consecration'. But the Council would not have it. There were three places of worship in Geneva, the churches of St. Peter, St. Gervais and La Madeleine. Sermons were numerous and formed the essence of pastoral labour, since they were preached every day. The Lord's Supper was celebrated four times a year although Calvin would have liked a celebration every Sunday. Each week the pastors from town and country met for study of the Bible together and for mutual admonition. This was the Congregation, which brought together what was named the Company of pastors.

The Ordinances of 1541 laid down also the basis of the

educational system. There would be at Geneva a school
of theology for the training of pastors and a college for the
teaching of small children. We have here in embryonic
form the future Academy of 1559.

The elders, whose task it was to watch over the life of
the members of the Church and to admonish them in
loving fashion, formed the Consistory. It was composed of
twelve elders, two chosen by the Smaller Council, four
from the Council of the Sixty and six from the Council of
the Two Hundred, all nominated by the Smaller Council
and not by the Church. These elders had seats in the
Consistory with the pastors and met one day per week
under the Chairmanship of one of the syndics.

What was the task of the Consistory? This creation of
Calvinism has been much criticized; it has been considered as an inquisitorial institution, indiscreet, leading
inevitably to Pharisaism and to hypocrisy. It has been
viewed as the weapon in Calvin's hands with which he
imposed an unbearable tyranny on the city. What are we
to think of these criticisms?

Our own age has completely neglected church discipline.
Believers carry on their lives in an individualistic fashion
and consider (I am speaking here of the better ones) that
they have to give an account to nobody and are responsible
only to the judgment of God. Any remark by a pastor
or an elder would be considered as an intrusion into the
domain of their private lives. In our churches in France
there is no longer any check on those who come to the
Lord's Supper. Each person approaches the holy table in
the light of his own spiritual responsibility. Granted,
moralizing interpretations (far removed from Calvinist
thought) on the dignity of the communicant have kept too
many believers away from the Communion for the re-estab-

lishment of ecclesiastical discipline to be possible or even necessary. But it remains no less true that the omission of discipline is a mark of our having given up a corporate conception of the Church. If the present-day movement in the direction of a Christian community becomes stronger, the re-establishing of some form of order in the Church will become inevitable. The preaching of the gospel is like the soul of the Church and discipline is like the joints which unite the members of the Church in one body.[1] The proclamation of the Word is the dynamic element by which the Church conquers; the work of the elders is the preservation of this Church through warnings, through recalling it to order and through private admonition. The task of the Consistory in Calvinist thought was thus to watch over the practice of received doctrine, to recall the hesitant, to admonish the weak and the fallen, in order to win them back rather than to frighten them away. In fact, Consistorial discipline was a magnificent cure of souls exerted in common by pastors and laymen over the weaker members of the Church.

The thought which lies behind the establishment of Consistorial discipline is that of the honour of God. The body of Christ must not be infected by rotting members. The enemies of the Church must not be able to poke fun at the so-called disciples of Christ. Especially must the sacrament of fellowship and love be preserved from profanation by those partaking who have not forgiven others that have trespassed against them, or who do not obey the Lord.

At the time when Geneva was under the rule of a bishop, this control was exercised by confession and absolution, which were obligatory for those who wished to communicate. Having shaken off the yoke of Rome

[1] Cf. *Inst.*, IX, xii, 2.

however, the people might not be left to their own devices. The oversight of the parishes would be entrusted to the elders who would keep an eye on the life of the believers, not to judge them but to warn them 'in gentleness and kindness'.

But what happens to all things human was to happen to the Consistory. It was quickly threatened by hardening of the arteries and the deadness of routine. The offences with which it had to concern itself were sometimes serious, for example adultery and fornication, and sometimes petty. Certain cases which the Consistory had to consider have often been quoted to make it a laughing-stock. 'Against a widow who was accustomed to use the prayer *requiescat in pace* over the tomb of her husband; having one's fortune told by the gypsies, having laughed during the sermon, having sung a satirical song against Calvin.' But it would be wrong to judge the activity of the Consistory from a few curious cases, just as it would be in our day wrong to judge the morality of a town on the basis of the drunkards taken into the cells, or by the quarrelsome wives about whom we can read each day in our newspaper.

But it has been said that Calvin used excommunication as a means of domination. 'Thus, by a stroke of genius, transforming the religious mystery of communion into a means of power and pressure.'[1] The accusation is a tremendous one and it is false. Firstly because excommunication was very rarely pronounced by the Consistory and only on the occasion of notorious scandals. Secondly because excommunication did not create a civil prohibition, a 'social and economic boycott', as Zweig affirms. It was a religious decision, purely religious, and one which had as its aim the bringing back of the sinner, making him come to himself, so leading to his repentance and his return to God. Here again we must quote the *Institutes*. Calvin

[1] Stephan Zweig: *Castellion contre Calvin*, Paris, 1936, p. 35.

distinguished between lesser faults and serious faults, between offences and crimes:

'For it is not right to employ the same severity towards an offence as we do towards a crime. It is sufficient to use verbal reproof, nay, sweet and paternal reproof, not calculated to crush and embitter the sinner but to bring him to himself in order that he may rejoice more at having been corrected rather than become grieved over it. But crimes must be punished more severely, for it is not enough to correct in words a man who has offended the Church by his bad example. He deserves to be deprived of the communion of the Lord's Supper until he has shown signs of repentance. . . . This danger is always to be avoided, as St. Paul commands—that the man who is punished should not be overwhelmed by sadness, for by this means we should be making a poison out of a cure. . . . Since excommunication has this aim of bringing sinners back to repentance and the removal of all bad examples, in order that the name of Jesus Christ be not blasphemed and others be not led to evil-doing by following them, it will be easy to decide just how far severity should go and at what point it must stop.'[1]

With this passage in which so much pastoral care of souls is evident and so much respect for the honour of God, we are far removed from the clerical Machiavellianism which Calvin's enemies attribute to him. They lack the spiritual understanding which discovers in the Reformer's activity something other than jealous ambition, and the thirst for dominion, with which his opponents have taxed him down the centuries.

On this point of excommunication conflicts were to rage at Geneva between Calvin and the civil government from 1541 to 1564. But on what were they centred? Did Calvin

[1] *Inst.*, IV, xii, 8.

want to dominate the city Council? Did he wish to impose his will on the magistrates? Certainly not. But in this strange sixteenth-century situation, inherited from the mediaeval conception of the temporal dominion of the bishop, constant confusion arises between the spiritual power and the civil power. It is the magistrate who nominates the elders of the Church, the magistrate who desires to pronounce excommunication or cancel it, the magistrate who aspires to have the last word on all matters, including those in the ecclesiastical realm. Against this pretension which has been given the name 'caesaro-papism' in historical studies, Calvin vehemently protests. He affirms the distinction of the two powers, he refuses the magistrate the right to pronounce ecclesiastical judgments; and it was on this question, as we have seen above, that he was hounded out of Geneva. It was on this question that he took up the fight again on his return. He wished to establish this distinction between spiritual and civil power. The Consistory cannot pronounce civil penalties. Its task is to warn the erring on the religious level and to admonish them by refusing them partici-pation in the Lord's Supper if they continue in their faults. But it is the magistrate's task to pronounce if there is a case for civil judgment, and to send to the 'crotton' (that is, to the cell or to the dungeon), or in more serious cases, into exile. The Consistory only uses 'the spiritual sword of the Word'. Calvin always affirmed the independence of the two realms and refused to give in when the magis-trate wished to impose his will in decisions which depend only on spiritual authority.

We must look at an example of these conflicts and of Calvin's refusal to give in to an intrusion by the civil power into affairs of the Church.

Philibert Berthelier was one of the most popular men

in Geneva, the son of a patriot who had resisted Savoyard domination in 1519. He led a loose life and found the warnings of the Consistory unbearable. He had been excommunicated and justly. But at a difficult juncture, at the time when the Servetus affair (which we shall examine later) was arising, he wished to profit from the fact that Calvin's opponents in the Council had the majority by asking the Council for their authorization to partake in the Lord's Supper. He was refusing the ecclesiastical decision of the Consistory and wanting to obtain from the civil jurisdiction the right to communicate. The Council decided that, if Berthelier 'felt that he was clear in his conscience and capable of receiving the Lord's Supper, he might take it, and that it be left to him to decide whether to do so or not'. This was to take the matter out of the hands of the ecclesiastical authorities in a domain which was purely that of the Church.

Calvin protested. He declared, 'that he had decided to die rather than to profane so shamefully the Lord's Supper, and that he would die a hundred times rather than submit to such shameful mockery'. The Council upheld its decision 'notwithstanding the matters and remonstrances put forward by Calvin'. And the Supper was to be celebrated the next day.

On Sunday morning Calvin went up into the pulpit of St. Peter's Cathedral. Before a crowd which knew the full story, he began the sermon which preceded the Supper. He declared that he did not recognize the decision of the Council; he denied it the right to intervene in a case which concerned the Church; he cried, 'I shall follow the example of Chrysostom and I shall rather allow myself to be killed than hold out with this hand the holy things of God to scorners under censure.'

Then he came down from the pulpit and took up his

position behind the holy table. 'There was a deathly silence. There he stood behind the table, this pale, thin, broken, worn-out figure, seeming to be nothing more than a gust of wind, but whose smouldering, fevered gaze sought out in the crowd the excommunicated man. There was a solemn, agonizing wait . . . and Berthelier did not come forward. The Council, moved despite everything by the adjurations of Calvin, had secretly informed the offender that it would be better if he would abstain from taking the Supper for the present.'

Calvin had triumphed. But he was worn out, and when he went back into the pulpit that afternoon he left suspended over the people's heads the threat of his departure. 'I must lay before you that I do not know whether this is the last sermon that I must preach at Geneva; not that I am taking leave on my own account; but if I am forced to do what is not right before God, it is impossible for me to proceed further, as far as I am concerned.'

The independence of the Church was saved. Some have called this dictatorship. We prefer to call it dignity.

Consequently, when we speak of the theocracy inaugurated by Calvin at Geneva we must not think, as has too often been thought, of a domination by the Reformer of the city's life, and make of Calvin a kind of Cardinal of Richelieu, taking all decisions of State as though he were a sovereign, and sometimes allowing the soldier's armour to appear beneath the folds of his red robe. Calvin was a preacher of the Word of God. Ceaselessly from the lofty pulpit he repeated, and through his writings declared, that the will of God as it is revealed in the holy Scriptures must be obeyed, down to its very details. He would not permit this will to be disregarded or this rule of doctrine and of life to be misunderstood. This is not so much a theocracy as a 'bibliocracy'.

Lastly, the Ordinances of 1541 established a fourth order: the deacons, by which we are to understand those who were entrusted with the distribution of alms or who took care of the sick in hospital. Thus the Church rediscovered the four fundamental activities through which, in the Acts of the Apostles, the activity of believers was displayed in the early Christian community: preaching (Acts ii. 42), care for the poor (Acts vi. 3), the rule of the parishes (Acts xiv. 23), and teaching (Acts xviii. 24).

With this teaching in mind, at the end of November, 1541, Calvin wrote the catechism called the Geneva Catechism in the space of a few days, some say within eight days. This second catechism by Calvin is distinct from that of 1537, of which we have spoken earlier, firstly in form and secondly in arrangement. Formally, it is a catechism in dialogue, whilst the *Instruction* of 1537 took the form of an exposition. The minister questions and the child replies. It is different, too, as far as arrangement is concerned, for Calvin, who in 1537 had followed the plan of Luther's Catechism and had dealt successively with the law, faith, prayer and baptism and the Lord's Supper (the five points of the Catechism), now modified the classical sequence of teaching and dealt first with faith, then with the law, and finally with prayer and the sacraments. The reasons for this change are theological. For Luther, the part played by the law is above all to convince man of his sin. 'The commandments teach man his malady in so far as he sees and feels what he can do and what he cannot do, what he can avoid and what he cannot avoid, and he recognizes himself as a sinner and an evil-doer. Then faith is presented. . . . This is why we place in the first position the teaching of the commandments and the confession of our sin, our iniquity, that is to say, the spiritual sickness which prevents our doing anything or avoiding anything as we ought.'[1]

Luther's conception of law has its source in well-known passages in the Epistle to the Romans (vii. 13), where the apostle Paul declares that the law gives the knowledge of sin and drives it to its final and most serious stage. But this use of the law, sometimes called a theological use, is not the only one. The law remains God's will and is the norm of the Christian's life, of the man who has been regenerated. 'It shows us the goal to which we must aspire, in order that each of us, following the grace of God which has been given to him, might try continually to strain towards it and to advance day by day.' This positive role of the law is better displayed when the explanation of the Decalogue follows that of the Apostles' Creed. Moreover this was the order followed by Bucer in his catechisms and here again we have a clear indication of the Strasbourg Reformer's influence on Calvin.

As soon as he returned to Geneva, Calvin was keen to put a catechism into the hands of the children with all speed. Hence he drew it up in a few days. 'On my return from Strasbourg,' he said in his *Farewell to the Pastors of Geneva*, 'I produced the catechism with all haste, for I never wished to accept the ministry unless they swore to keep to these two points, that is, to maintain the use of the catechism and discipline; and as I wrote it, they came and got the pieces of paper which were a hand's breadth in width and took them to the printers. Although Master Pierre Viret was in the town, do you think that I ever showed him anything of it? I never had leisure to do this, and indeed I had sometimes thought of setting my hand to it if I had had the leisure.'

We no longer possess this 1542 edition. But we may

[1] Luther's Preface to the *Kurze Form der Zehn Gebote*.

assume that it was identical with that of 1545, published
at Geneva by Jean Gérard. At the time of the first edition,
however, the catechism was not divided into fifty-five sec-
tions or fifty-five Sundays, for it was explained every Sunday in a meeting which was not reserved for children alone.
Rather than a pedagogic work fitted for a mind which is
still at the child's stage, it is a work of doctrine, a remark-
ably clear exposition of the faith. Karl Barth sees in it a
doctrinal basis, a work which forms a rallying-point for
all those who are willing to confess the Reformed faith.
It must be noted, however, that Calvin excluded from it
the doctrines that were more difficult to teach, such as that
of predestination.[1]

Despite his numerous tasks—for he could write in
January, 1542, 'since my arrival here I can only remember
having been granted two hours in which no-one has come
and disturbed me'—Calvin nevertheless did not cease to
produce printed theological works. In 1543 he published
the third Latin edition of the *Institutes* which appeared at
Strasbourg and which was soon translated into French
(second French edition 1545). This edition embodied the
additions to the text of 1539 (Latin) and 1541 (French).
It was made up of twenty-one chapters instead of seventeen.

As early as 1541 he published at Geneva his *Little
Treatise on the Lord's Supper*, which he had doubtless
prepared at Strasbourg. He wrote it straight down in
French, having proved by his translation of the *Institutes*
into his mother tongue that great theological themes,
hitherto set forth in Latin only, could be expressed in the
vulgar tongue and become accessible to all. Thus Calvin
pioneered the way for those who wrote theological books
in French after him, François de Sales, Pascal, Bossuet.

[1] K. Barth: *Parole de Dieu et Parole Humaine*, p. 216.

INSTITVTIO
CHRISTIANÆ
religionis,

Joanne Caluino authore.

Additi funt nuper duo Indices, antè ab Auguftino
Marlorato collecti:quorum prior res præcipuas,
pofterior in ea expofitos copiofiffimè facræ Scri-
pturæ locos continet.

Introite per arctâ portâ:quoniam lata eft porta & fpatiofa via quæ abducit in exitium, Matth. 7.13.

GENEVÆ,

Ex officina Francifci Perrini,

M. D. LXIX.

Title page of the 1569 edition of the *Institutes*

Granted, his language retained the basic framework of Latin. We are still conscious that it is strongly shaped by the vocabulary and syntax of the Latin language. His Latin is clearer and more incisive than his French, yet what spontaneity, what richness of vocabulary and what life there is in it! We may quote the evaluation of Bossuet as he compared the style of the two Reformers. 'Let us grant him then, since he desires it so much, this great honour of having written as well as any man in his century. Let us even put him, if you wish, above Luther. For although Luther had something more original and more powerful about him, Calvin, a man of lesser genius, seems to have been the deeper student. Luther was supreme as a speaker, but Calvin's pen was more correct, especially in Latin; and his style, which was more sober, was also more coherent and more polished. Each excelled at speaking the language of his own country.'[1] From this assessment the conclusion is quickly drawn that Calvin's style is sober. Now Bossuet simply said that it was more sober than Luther's. The man who speaks of Calvin's style as a sober style, simply shows that he has not read two pages of the *Institutes*. Vivid words abound there, and we not infrequently meet with expressions which are sometimes quite brutal. Let us read at random, 'A worthy Father once gave a very good reply to one of those who, in scornful pleasantry, demanded what God was busy with before He created the world, by saying "He was building hell for the curious". This warning both serious and severe should quell all disorderly inquisitiveness which tickles many people and even drives them on to speculations which are as harmful as they are crooked. In short, let us remember that the invisible God whose

[1] Bossuet, *Histoire des Variations des Eglises protestantes*, Bk. IX, para. 81.

wisdom, virtue and justice are incomprehensible, has put before our eyes the story of Moses as a mirror, in which He wishes us to see the shining of His own image. For just as eyes which are infected or dim with age, or dulled by any other fault or illness, cannot see clearly, unless they are helped by spectacles, so our stupidity is such that unless Scripture urges us to seek God we should give up straight away. If those who allow themselves to gibe and to babble on shamelessly take no warning now, they will feel too late in their own terrible ruin how much more useful it would have been to them to contemplate the whole vast extent of God's secret counsel in all reverence, than to spew out their blasphemies and darken heaven.'[1]

After being prepared at Strasbourg then, the *Little Treatise on the Lord's Supper* was published at Geneva in 1541. As its title indicates, it is a small treatise, of some forty pages. Even before his conversion Calvin had been troubled and, perhaps, halted for a moment on the road to evangelical faith by the controversy between Luther and Zwingli on the doctrine of the Lord's Supper. Their meeting at the Marburg Colloquy (1529) could not conclude with any agreement. Ten years had passed. After a time Calvin takes up the question again. He does so with simplicity and depth and we have said above that Luther doubtless viewed this work favourably. It is a restatement 'briefly and nevertheless clearly', to use the author's own expressions. We shall give a résumé of it in broad outline.

God who, by baptism, has received us into His house as His children continues in His capacity as Father towards us by giving us spiritual nourishment for our souls. Now Scripture tells us that the bread of our souls, the bread of life, is Jesus Christ. There is life only in God and He has appointed Jesus Christ to be the One who transmits this

[1] *Inst.*, I, xiv, 1.

fullness of life. 'Our souls have no other pasture than Jesus Christ.' This life which is in Christ is given us now by means of the Word and the sacrament. The Lord signs and seals in our consciences the promises of His gospel by means of the sacrament, which is a visible confirmation of His Word. A further task of the Supper is to lead us to praise God (this is the sense of the term *eucharist*, thanksgiving, by which it is sometimes designated), and to permit us thus to show forth our brotherly love towards other believers.

What are these promises which the Supper confirms for us? Those of our salvation. In us there is no righteousness, we are all full of sin and iniquity, and our conscience accuses us. The judgment of God weighs heavily upon us. 'We are therefore already in the abyss of death unless our kind God rescues us from it.' Now the Supper is given to us as a mirror in which we may contemplate our Lord Jesus Christ, crucified to do away with our sins and raised again to bring us back into the eternal life of heaven. In the Supper our Lord is given us. Here Calvin employs the strongest terms to denote the reality of this gift. 'All the usefulness that we must seek in the Supper is nullified unless Jesus Christ is given us as substance and foundation of all. That having been decided, we shall confess without any doubt that to deny that Jesus Christ is truly communicated to us in the Supper is to render this holy sacrament frivolous and useless, which is an accursed blasphemy unworthy to be heard.' This communion in the body and blood of the Lord, that is to say, in His humanity in which He suffered for us and made satisfaction in our stead, is prefigured to us by visible signs, but in such a way that the internal substance of the sacraments is joined with these visible signs. Calvin does not hesitate to use the word 'substance', charged though it be with theological ambiguity. We meet it at least ten times in the course of the treatise. As another example: 'Jesus Christ gives us in the Supper the very substance of His body and blood in order that we might be fully possessors of it, and possessing it, be partakers in all His riches.' He uses the word then, not in the theological sense but in the general sense of 'fundamental reality'.

But how is this gift of the fullness of Christ given to us through the visible sign? Here we meet with the great Calvinist doctrine of the action of the Holy Spirit. The presence of Christ in the Supper is a *spiritual* presence, which means a presence which is a work of the Holy Spirit. 'We must realize that this takes place by the secret, miraculous power of God, and that the Spirit of God is the blessing in this participation, for which cause it is called spiritual.' 'To understand rightly the usefulness of the Supper we must not think that our Lord warns us, stirs us up and inflames our hearts only by the external signs. For the principal matter is that He is active in us by His Holy Spirit within.'

Then Calvin broaches the question of the worthiness of the communicant. Who must communicate? Who may communicate? The only conditions that Christ imposes are repentance and faith, the feeling of our own weakness and faith in His grace alone. We should come frequently to the Lord's table and often. Calvin was elsewhere to make clear what he meant by this 'often'—once a week at the Sunday morning service of worship. For him the Supper is an integral part of this worship.[1]

Calvin then refutes various erroneous conceptions of the Supper in the Roman Church. To affirm that the Supper is 'a sacrifice by which we acquire remission of our sins before God is an utterly intolerable blasphemy'. For

[1] *Inst.*, IV, xvii, 43, 44.

this would be to misunderstand the unique character of the death of Jesus on the cross. He is the only High Priest, through whose intercessions we are brought back into the grace of the Father. This would be to deprive Him of His honour and to insult Him. Calvin also rejects transubstantiation, for the very idea of a sacrament, i.e., a 'sign', demands that the material bread should remain as a sign, and not be abolished in order to be replaced by any other substance. Likewise communion in one kind alone must be condemned, for this deprives the faithful of the sign of the blood which was shed for the remission of sins. Jesus said, 'Drink ye all of it,' and the arrogance of the pope is such that he dares to say, 'Do not all drink of it.'

In the final section Calvin alludes to the quarrel about the sacraments between Luther and Zwingli which so sadly divided the Reformation in its early years and which still divides it—and that without any real theological reason, we dare to affirm. Calvin was grieved at this painful division and made every effort to heal the breach. He showed that in rejecting transubstantiation Luther continued to affirm that the bread remained united with the body of Christ, without giving to his affirmation even the rough outlines of a reasoned theological doctrine. 'But he did it as it were out of constraint, because he could in no other way explain what he intended.' Calvin here alludes to Luther's letter to the Christians at Strasbourg,[1] in which the Reformer maintains that it would have greatly pleased him to have found some good means of denying the bodily, substantial presence of Christ in the bread, because nothing would have better served his purpose of harming the papacy. But he believed that he had to stick by the literal sense of the words at the institution of the Supper, 'This is my body'. He summed up his position in

[1] *Martin Luther's Werke*, Weimar edition, XV, p. 394.

the well-known formula, 'I believe with Wycliffe that the
bread remains, and with the sophists (the schoolmen) that
the body is there' (*Babylonian Captivity*). Luther lacked
any theological expression which would have allowed him
to affirm the reality of Christ's presence without either
falling straight into the substantialism of the Roman
theory, or into the excessive spiritualism of the Anabaptists
after the manner of Carlstadt.

On the other hand, Zwingli and Œcolampadius at
Marburg, fearing the Roman theory of transubstantiation
and its consequences, particularly the adoration of the
holy sacrament and its 'damnable idolatry', insisted on the
presence of the glorified Christ in heaven and His absence
as far as the earthly elements of bread and wine were
concerned. Zwingli's argument, which relies on the
ascension of the Lord, has in fact never been refuted.
Calvin, the theologian of transcendence, was to take his
stand on it with complete confidence. But at Marburg,
although the object of the meeting was to bring about
unity, Zwingli seemed to harden his position rather than
to soften its corners. And Luther, who saw in the Swiss
Reformers men who had received into their churches the
Anabaptist Carlstadt, and who himself clung to a literalist
position, believed his interlocutors much further from
him than they really were. 'Though they [Zwingli and
Œcolampadius] made great play with this idea [the
matter of the presence of the glorified Christ in heaven],
they forgot to show what kind of presence of Jesus Christ
in the Supper must be believed in, and what communion
in His body and blood we receive in it. So that Luther
thought that their aim was to leave nothing more than
naked signs without their *spiritual substance*.' We underline
these last two words, for they define Calvin's own position.
He affirms the presence of Christ in the Supper but while

adopting the term 'substance' he somehow sublimates it
by recalling, through the very term *spiritual*, that there is
no reality in the sacrament apart from the action of the
Holy Spirit. If Luther had openly said that he rejected
Roman transubstantiation and if Zwingli had openly said
that for him the reality is really joined to the sign, there
might have been an agreement. 'Both parties failed in not
having the patience to listen to the other.' Very close to
Calvin's heart was the great hope that he would see the
controversy over the Supper vanish and the unity of the
Reformation appear, this unity for which, as he wrote to
Cranmer, 'I am ready to cross ten oceans.'

Unfortunately, in this hope he was disappointed. In
1549 Calvin established with Henry Bullinger, Zwingli's
successor at Zurich, *An Agreement on the Sacraments*. This
agreement contained twenty-six articles, out of which
twenty are devoted to an exposition of the doctrine of
sacraments in general, and six deal with the Lord's Supper.
One is struck by the Christological emphasis in this work.
Here, for example, is article six: 'This is the spiritual
communion which we have with the Son of God, when
He, who dwells in us by His Spirit, makes us partakers of
all the riches which dwell in Him. It is to testify to this
communion that both the preaching of the gospel and the
use of the sacraments has been ordained for us.' The
sacrament is therefore a sign, a testimony of the spiritual
communion that Christ grants us to have with Him.

But the quarrel on the sacraments was to be sparked off
again by article twenty-four, which was drawn up in these
terms: 'By this, not only is the foolish imagination of the
papists reproved, in that they delude people into believing
that the bread is transubstantiated into the flesh of Christ,
but so, too, are all other clumsy imaginations and frivolous
subtleties which are derogatory to the heavenly glory of

Christ, or are not consonant with the truth of His human nature. Now we do not believe that it is any less absurd to shut up Jesus Christ in the form of bread or to join Him with the bread, than to say that the bread is transubstantiated into His body.'

By this latter phrase Calvin was giving his judgment that the Lutheran doctrine of consubstantiation, affirming the simultaneous presence of the substance of the bread and the substance of the body of Christ, was as absurd as the Roman doctrine of transubstantiation. A Lutheran theologian, Joachim Westphal of Hamburg, accepted the challenge, and there followed a long and painful controversy into which we shall not enter here. But we must note the distressing outcome. The Christianity which sprang from the Reformation was to remain divided on the question of the Lord's Supper, and it has remained so until today. Let us hope that the time will shortly come when these quarrels will be forgotten and when, with all recognizing the affirmation of Christ's real presence, the unity of the Reformation Church will be established.

Thus by his daily preaching at St. Peter's, by his theological instruction, by his treatises, Calvin was gradually clarifying the doctrine of the Reformation and giving it a structure. The Reformation was coming out of its first stage as a humanistic or reforming movement which had been the hallmark of Lefèvre d'Etaples, of Marguerite d'Angoulême and those who formed a group around her, Guillaume Briçonnet, Michel d'Arande, Gérard Roussel. Persecution had come and obliged those who wished to break with superstition to take a clear stand. A separation was necessary unless they were to be unfaithful to their convictions and to take the side of the persecutors.

This brings us to speak of a group of Calvin's writings which can be dated between 1543 and 1549 and which were brought together under the title: *Superstitions which must be avoided* (*De vitandis superstitionibus*). First came, in 1543, a *Little Treatise showing what a faithful man must do, knowing the truth of the gospel, when he is among the papists.* Then in 1544, following the sermons which had provoked this first treatise, came a second: *The Excuse of John Calvin to the Nicodemites on the complaint that they make about his excessive harshness.* Let us stop for a moment over this latter work.

'Nicodemites' was the name given to those who seemed to be afraid to take a stand, thus following the example of Nicodemus who had come by night to see Jesus, doubtless for fear of compromising his position. 'There were at that time in France', Beza tells us, 'a certain number of people who, having fallen into superstition at the very beginning out of fear, had in the event found so comfortable a path that they denied that there was any sin in adhering to the true religion while at the same time continuing to participate physically in the ceremonies used in the Church of Rome. This extremely pernicious error had been condemned in earlier days by the Fathers. Calvin, whom these people reproached for his excessive severity, refuted them in his turn in a most pungent piece of writing. Then, on the authority of the view of certain most learned theologians, Melanchthon, Bucer, Peter Martyr, and those of the Church of Zurich, he reprimanded them so strongly that from that time onwards all pious folk detested the name Nicodemite. This was the name given to those who sheltered their error under the example of this holy man.'

How are we to explain the attitude of the Nicodemites? Was it not above all else their fear of creating a schism, of tearing the Church apart, and the hope they had of achieving a Reformation without a break? But the harshness of persecution removed this hope from them. The dream of a victory for the gospel within the bounds of the established Church was vanishing away. Farel, who had learned from Lefèvre d'Etaples, and with him known Gérard Roussel (who later became Bishop of Oloron in Béarn) and Michel d'Arande (who took charge of the diocese of Saint-Paul-Trois-Châteaux in Dauphiné), was severe on his former fellow-pupils. He wrote: 'those who direct the movement in France must be exhorted not to perish in their sins. Far from confessing their error, after having failed to appreciate the truth, they are reaching the point of setting up their impiety as a veritable creed. . . . There are some who are falling because they were not firmly grounded enough in the faith. They are only a small group. Others, in greater numbers, have come out of the trial more faithful than ever. But I know many more who, at the very same time that they are dabbling in the mud and imagining that they are doing no harm, have finally lost all piety and have made shipwreck of their faith. These latter people make it their sole task to please men. They are carried in whatsoever direction the wind blows and they are a stumbling-block to all. . . . I have realized with great grief that there are no worse people in France, no greater obstacle to piety, than these who have the reputation of siding with the Word of God and being well disposed to the gospel.'

Calvin gives what is virtually the same explanation. 'What shall I say of those who, after having tasted the gift of God, instead of opposing this insufferable tyranny with all their force as they ought, conceal on the contrary, despite their real opinions, the sad state of the [persecuted] Church. Out of consideration for their reputation or for their wealth they suffer in silence these iniquitous judgments, and they would regard it as dishonour if they were to be the objects of the least suspicion. Moreover, in order not to expose themselves to the reproach of impiety, they allege that the doctrine of the gospel causes so many scandals. They go shouting to anyone who will listen to them, that public peace is endangered by those whom they call the new followers of the gospel, and though they are very eloquent, on the other hand their lives are but little conformed to the gospel.'

Calvin sets against these compromises and this refusal to protest against the harsh persecution which was raging against the preachers of evangelical doctrines in France, the obligation of absolute sincerity and complete conformity between personal faith and external practice. We may not separate the attitude of the body and the conviction of the soul, because body and soul both belong to the Lord, both are called to glorify God. One cannot follow Roman ceremonies externally and claim to be keeping one's soul pure from idolatry. God demands the piety of the whole life, not a private piety.

Calvin takes to task the various groups of these waverers in turn. First, those who attract large congregations, preach the gospel, and proclaim some elements of pure doctrine, but will not go the whole way in their preaching. Then these 'fastidious reverend gentlemen', that is high ecclesiastical dignitaries and fawning abbots, 'who are quite content to have the gospel and to chat about it happily and merrily with the ladies, provided that that does not prevent them living as they see fit. I classify these spoilt darlings of the court with ladies who have never learnt to be anything but pampered and, for this reason, are incapable of understanding anything apart from compliments paid to their elegance. I am in no way amazed if the whole lot of them band together against me as if they had taken a great oath, and all condemn my excessive severity with one voice. I seem to hear them saying, "Let's have no more talk of Calvin, he is too inhuman. What! if we were to believe him, he would not only make us beggars but he would lead us straight to the stake. Is there any need to hurry us on in this way? If he wants everyone to be like him, if he is grieved to see us better off than he is, what does that matter to us? We are doing very nicely here, let him stay where he is and leave everyone else in peace." The conclusion is that I don't know what the world is like. When they have told each other all sorts of flattering tales, they think that they have taken vengeance on me. Very well. But what will they do before God to whom I refer their case, and who will summon them by the sound of the trumpet [i.e. to appear before the last judgment]? A reverend gentleman may well merrily defy the crucifix and live a fast life in feasting, gaming, dancing and all sorts of gallantry, at its expense. For a crucifix is nothing but a little idol. But God will not be mocked in this way. . . . Instead of their holding forth continually against me and having a good laugh at my warnings, I should like to get them to think that one day they must appear before God to be judged by this same Word that I set before them now. For my part, I have not been hired to tickle their fancy.'[1]

A third category is that of the philosophers who, being idealists of a sort, believed the truth of God to be separable from religious practice which, in itself, was indifferent. The fourth is that of the merchants and the common people who want only one thing, that is, to be left in peace.

For these various opponents of his severity, Calvin recalls the word of Christ. 'Whosoever will save his life

[1] *Op. Calv.*, VI, pp. 598–600.

shall lose it: and whosoever will lose his life for my sake shall find it.' And he concludes: 'If the faithful of the early Church had said as much [as the Nicodemites], what would have become of Christianity? Would it not have been crushed and swept away before it came into existence? ... All the theology of the ancient martyrs lay in knowing that there is one God who must be adored, that in Him alone man's entire confidence must be centred, that the true service which He requires is adoring Him and calling upon His name. ... Their knowledge of these beliefs was not so lofty that they could present them as the results of subtle and detailed deductions, but they held them in all simplicity. Yet withal they would run with a merry heart to the fire or to any other death to which they were condemned. Nay, the women even took their children thither. We who are mightily learned and can so cleverly discuss all these matters, we do not know what it is to testify to the truth of God in the hour of need and to prove our Christianity.'

It was by strong remonstrances of this kind that Calvin was able to bring the emergent Reformation movement in France through the crisis of Nicodemism. The break did take place, and very painfully. But this was the price of upholding the truth which had been recovered. A clear stand had to be taken in the face of both a vague humanism and of superstitious popery. Through the courageous advice given in his printed writings, Calvin enabled the Church of the Word of God to be set up, despite those who persecuted or compromised.

But now, after 1549, the danger was no longer just an external threat from France; it was emerging within the Church of Geneva itself. And here Calvin was to face some hard fighting for the truth.

CHAPTER X

THE STRUGGLE FOR THE TRUTH

THE difficulties that had beset Calvin from the very start in giving to the Reformation a framework and a constitution were to become no less as the years went by. We must not be surprised at that. Among the people and the Councillors of the town there always remained those who gave little support to the Reformer's desire to see the triumph of Christian morality and biblical doctrine, and who wished to shake off the yoke of one whom they regarded as an intruder. Representatives of old Genevan families were ill-disposed towards these refugees, these Frenchmen who came laying down the law amongst them. Now the only resources Calvin had to hand, as we have already said, were those of his spiritual authority as a preacher. This background of struggle gave to his words a certain hardness and a certain severity, a controversial note for which he has often been blamed.

We must go further. Calvin believed that the man who denied revealed truth was more guilty in the eyes of society than the man who attacked his neighbour's life, his honour or his property. In the Ten Commandments of the law of God, two 'tables' are generally distinguished. These are the two tablets of the law often represented in Bible pictures. It will be seen that the four commandments of the first table make clear our duty towards God and the six commandments of the second table our duties towards our neighbour. Now Calvin believed that those who disobeyed the commandments of the first table should be punished by the magistrate just as much as those who disobeyed those of the second. Idolatry is a crime, heresy is a crime. They must be chastised and repressed in the same way as murder, adultery and theft. For the man who corrupts the soul is much more guilty than he who aims only at the body. Moreover, he is doing his very worst to assail the glory of God.

In our twentieth century we are very far from these ideas, and there is no question of returning to them. This would be impossible. At the expense of grievous suffering, Christendom—persecuted now under those of one persuasion and now under those of another, according to the age and the country—has learnt that there can be no constraint in the realm of religion. Freedom of conscience is freedom to affirm and also to deny. Freedom of the soul is the condition of sincerity; and there can be no faith without sincerity, for faith is the most personal step a man can take, involving the whole of his being. Lack of sincerity in faith is the most shameful hypocrisy. Now the fear of punishment can lead to pretence, and force a man to hypocrisy.

Among those whom Calvin fought, we must first mention Castellion. Sébastien Châtillon, usually known as Castellion on account of his Latin name, was born in Bugey[1] in 1515. At Lyons he was a humanist; but then he went over to the Reformation and being obliged to flee from persecution, he went to Strasbourg in 1540. He was welcomed there into Calvin's house, which was a kind of little seminary, in which a few young students met around the author of the *Institution chrétienne* to be trained for the pastoral ministry. In this same year, 1540, Calvin wrote

[1] *Translator's note.* A district in Burgundy, at that time not French territory, but belonging to the Duke of Savoy.

to Bèza: 'If we would really make provision for the profit of the Church, we must call to the office of pastor people who will be able some day to take on the responsibility after us. Although I am young, yet when I see my weakness and bodily sickness, I am concerned for those who will come after us, as if I were already an old man.' Castellion stayed there only a few days, but his friendly feelings towards Calvin were whole-hearted, as was also his admiration.

Calvin's handwriting

Three months before Calvin's return to Geneva, Castellion had arrived in the town as principal of the college. From the educational point of view he did a fine job of work there. In 1543 he asked to be received as pastor at Vandœuvres, in Genevan territory. Calvin opposed his nomination for two reasons. First, Castellion had disputed the inspiration of the Song of Solomon and had expressed regret that it was in the canon of Holy Scripture, and, second, he had criticized Calvin's interpretation of the descent into hell mentioned in the Apostles' Creed.[1] Some may think these matters of little importance; but Calvin considered that doubt cast on the inspiration of a book of the Bible was an attack on the authority of Holy Scripture. One of the fundamental principles of the Reformation was being assailed. Castellion resigned his position a short time later to go to Basle. Calvin wrote him a testimonial in which he explained quite simply the pastors' reasons for refusing to receive him into the sacred ministry.

'So then, in order that no-one may suspect any other motive for Sebastian's departure, we wish it to be testified wherever he may go that he voluntarily resigned his office as principal of the college. These functions he had fulfilled in such a way that we judged him worthy of the sacred ministry. If he has not been admitted it is not on account of any kind of stain in his life, it is not by reason of any impious doctrine on any cardinal point of the faith which stood against it. It is simply the matter which we have just set out.' Castellion left for Basle and later we shall find him defending tolerance after the Servetus affair.

Of much greater interest is the man to whom we now turn, Jérôme Bolsec. Formerly a Carmelite, and a native of Paris, he had turned towards the Reformation. In his flight from persecution he had first taken refuge at the court of Renée of Ferrara. In 1550, we find him in the village of Veigy, in the neighbourhood of Geneva, as a doctor in the house of Jacques de Bourgogne, lord of Falais, a protestant noble who was a close friend of Calvin. The latter came from the Low Countries and had sided with the Reformation. He had been obliged to leave his estates and to retire first to Strasbourg in 1545, then to

[1] See *Inst.*, II, xvi, 11.

Basle, and finally to the Château de Veigy in 1548.

Bolsec was interested in theological questions and he often participated in the Congregation, the meeting of pastors at Geneva which took place every Friday. At each session there was a Bible study and those present could speak. Now Bolsec, who was in the main in agreement with Calvin's theology, was nevertheless very much opposed to the doctrine of predestination as the Reformer formulated it. In the Congregation of October 16, 1551, he made a violent attack on Calvin's views, maintaining that they were not in conformity with revealed truth and that their author was not a faithful interpreter of Holy Scripture. This amounted to an accusation of the gravest sort against the man who did not wish to have any other task at Geneva but that of preacher of the Word of God. Calvin embarked upon a lively discussion with him and at the end of the session a legal official approached Bolsec of his own accord and arrested him. This was an application of the principle that we have explained earlier of the possibility of the magistrate recognizing offences under the first table of the Decalogue.

The trial began. Bolsec defended himself by relying upon the doctrine of Melanchthon who had somewhat softened the doctrine of predestination. At his request the Smaller Council of Geneva asked the advice of neighbouring churches—Basle, Zurich, Berne and Neuchâtel. With the exception of the last-mentioned church, their opinion was that the doctrine of predestination was a difficult doctrine and that it would be better to try to bring about a reconciliation.

But on December 18, 1551, Calvin himself presided over a meeting of the Congregation on the 'eternal election of God', 'rejecting the error of a sower of false doctrine who had brazenly spewed out his poison'. And on the 23rd

of the same month Bolsec was officially banished from
Geneva.

We cannot think of setting out Calvin's long declaration
here. At the most we may sketch the broad outline of it.
Its tone is very animated. Bolsec is called a 'master
muddlehead', a 'charlatan', a 'cheeky beggar', a 'filthy
animal' and a 'pig'—compliments current in sixteenth-
century discussions. But the doctrine of predestination was
of so great importance, and its place in Calvin's work and
in Reformed thought is so primary, that without delaying
over the colourful style we shall now give a summary of
this declaration.

When we believe in Jesus Christ, Calvin maintained,
this does not come of ourselves, our own wills, our own
efforts, or our own decisions, but from the grace of God.
Faith is a gift of God. Now faith is not given to all men.
God Himself gives faith according to His will. Therefore
faith proceeds from a higher source than human will. It
springs from the free election of God by which He
chooses for salvation whomsoever He pleases.

In the Epistle to the Ephesians (i. 4, 5), St. Paul says
that God has chosen us in Christ from before the foundation of the world in order that we might be holy. He has
predestinated us in His love to become His children by
adoption. He has saved us and He has called us by a holy
calling, not according to works but according to His own
plan, according to His grace which has been given to us in
Jesus Christ before all the ages (2 Timothy i. 9).

It is true that God has regard to us in choosing us, but
what does He find in us? Nothing but wretchedness and
poverty, and hence He is moved with compassion and
shows mercy to whomsoever He pleases. And why? The
reason is not known to us; let it suffice us to know with

St. Paul that God has decided it according to His own secret counsel. He has chosen us in Christ because we are unworthy of it in ourselves. For in ourselves we are hated and worthy of God's abomination, but He sees us in His Son and thus He loves us.

This also is the sense of Romans viii. 29, 30. 'Those whom He foreknew, them He predestinated to be conformed to the image of His Son . . . and those whom He predestinated He also called; those whom He called He also justified and those whom He justified He also glorified.'

For fuller confirmation, let us come to John vi. 44. Jesus said: 'No man can come to me, except the Father which hath sent me draw him.' Now how is this 'drawing' exercised? God presents His word to all men, but He does not speak to all men within their hearts. If all do not come to Jesus Christ, this follows from the fact that all have not been taught of the Father (vi. 45). Therefore it does not derive from our virtue, dignity or merit, but from an act of God's pure grace.

When we come to Jesus Christ the fact is that we have been given to Him by the Father (John xvii. 6). In consequence Jesus receives into His care and protection those who have been given to Him by the Father and does not allow any of them to perish. When once we are in His care He will give us such strength that we shall persevere unto the end. Jesus said (John x. 29): 'No man shall snatch them out of my hand. The Father who has given me them is greater than all.'

Calvin comments thus: 'Here is what we must hold firmly in mind in order to do battle against so many temptations with which Satan attacks us to turn us aside. For otherwise, when we are assailed on all sides, when we have a hundred thousand deaths around us, where will be our strength and our resistance? Now God is invincible. Let us remember, then, that our salvation is certain. Why? Because it rests in the hand of God. And how are we assured of this? Because He has put this in the hand of our Lord Jesus who shows us that the Father who has chosen us will carry through His decree, effect it and complete it.'

From this we can understand how the doctrine provided such a source of assurance for Calvin and those of his time, the confessors of the faith who lay in prison or the martyrs who stood at the stake. *God is invincible.* And when they learnt in their dungeons that Bolsec was attacking the doctrine of election these men would tremble. Was their hope about to be undermined? For them these doctrines were not themes for discussion, but the grounds of a living certainty.

But let us continue with our exposition of the Reformed teaching. Those who entertain any other conception do not know what human nature really is. Let us consider a little what is in our nature and what can be got out of it if God had left it as it is. It is certain that our corruption is such that we cannot do other than evil. 'All the virtues of our nature are so many enemies opposed to God.' And so, when predestination is explained as God's foresight of our merits, the question is asked, 'What can God see in us if He leaves us as we are, unless it be detestable stinking filth?'

As we can see, Calvin's exposition is woven out of a number of biblical passages. That is his method. He does not demonstrate, he quotes. Or rather, his demonstration is simply and solely by means of quotations from Scripture.

Let us come now to objections, for numerous objections are made to this doctrine. 'A man must be a mere puppet of God before he can take this line.' But we must hold fast to this position, since God has said it and He wishes, by this doctrine, to test our humility.

Certain objectors will say: 'Yes, but I am afraid of making God unjust if I say that He does not elect all men.' But if we are forbidden to judge others, how much more are we forbidden to judge God, or to fear that He may be unjust. Is not this in some way to submit Him to our control? And what arrogance is that? One day when the books are opened we shall see why God has thus dealt with men. For the moment, let us content ourselves with saying that God is just. It seems to some that St. Paul was stuck for an answer when he said 'Man, who are you to raise yourself against God?' (Rom. ix. 20). On the contrary, this is the best reply that he could have made.

Others say that we could quite well do without this doctrine and teach simply faith and repentance. These latter wish to be wiser than God. It is true that we must observe due caution when we speak of election, and not go beyond our limits; but where do we set the bounds for our moderation? Is it in our wisdom, or in God Himself? It is therefore for God to declare to us that which He wishes to be known, and for us to receive it in humility.

Let us come to those who blaspheme openly and say, 'If God has elected whom He pleased, we are not going to take any trouble to live a holy life, since our salvation is outside our control.' Here Scripture replies: 'We are chosen with a holy calling so that, turning from our iniquity, we might be holy and without spot.' Let those who wish to blaspheme thus observe the example given by St. Augustine—that of Jesus Christ. For Jesus Christ is the mirror and pattern in which God has revealed the infinite treasures of His goodness. Behold Jesus Christ, true God and true Man. Now what has human nature deserved to be exalted to this wonderful dignity? The human nature in Him proceeds from Adam. He was conceived by His mother in a miraculous fashion, but yet He is of the race of Adam, otherwise He would not have been our Saviour at all. If He was not subject to the same corruption as us, that springs from God's wondrous grace. When we consider the extent of God's grace in the One who is our Head, must not each one of us look into our own heart and say to ourselves, 'God has chosen me. In me there was nothing which could be pleasing to Him; and yet, nevertheless He chose me for one of His own.' When we contemplate this grace we shall say with St. Paul: 'O the greatness . . .'

It will be noticed that Calvin does not enter into the philosophical realm and undertakes no examination of the relationship between grace and free-will. He remains on the biblical level, which is that of God's sovereign initiative in our salvation. He positions himself on Christological ground and contemplates, in Jesus Christ, the grace through which God took on human nature.

Calvin goes on to speak of the reprobates. For election of some involves in consequence the rejection of others. We might find it strange that God should reject those who are His creatures, but we must remember that in Adam we are all condemned and lost. God might well reject us all with justice. If He saves some, this is out of His pure lovingkindness. Can one blame Him for this lovingkindness? As the master of the house says in the parable: 'Do you see with an evil eye, because I am good?' (see Matthew xx. 15).

Agreed; but when God foresaw Adam did He not foresee what would happen? Yes indeed; but man was created righteous and good. If he stumbled, it was because he disobeyed God. If he committed such transgression,this comes from him and cannot be attributed to God.

Yet why did God permit it? Here, Calvin declares: 'We are not able to conceive this. It is an unfathomable gulf of mystery. Why should we hurl ourselves into it?'

Two more objections. It says in 1 Timothy ii. 4: 'God wishes all men to be saved.' This was one which Bolsec raised. If God wills that all should come to the knowledge of the truth, replies Calvin, why does He permit the world to have been blinded for so long a time? God does not speak of 'all' here in the universal sense, but in the general sense. 'All men' means here men of all conditions, princes and slaves, kings and subjects. The gospel is preached to all, but only those who are enlightened by God receive it. It was God who opened the heart of Lydia, the seller of purple (Acts xvi. 14), and the book of Acts says: 'All those who were ordained to salvation believed' (Acts xiii. 48). The gospel is indeed the power of God to save those who believe, but of ourselves we can only reject the gospel unless God enlightens us and calls us.

In conclusion Calvin broaches the important question of assurance of salvation. If someone says: 'And how do I know whether I am saved or lost?' he shows by that very question that he has never known what faith is, and what is the assurance that we must have in Jesus Christ. Do you wish to know whether you are elect? Look at yourself in Jesus Christ. For those who by faith are in true communion with Jesus Christ are, by this very fact, assured of belonging to the eternal election of God and of being His children. Whoever finds himself in Jesus Christ and a member of His body is assured of His salvation, for Jesus Christ is the foundation of our election and of our assurance.

We were anxious to give a fairly lengthy exposition of the broad outline of this work, for it is characteristic of Calvin's method: biblical truths, religious data. In later controversies Calvin was to harden his affirmations, and the last edition of the *Institutes* was to bear the marks of this hardening.

Bolsec was banished from Geneva but did not leave the Castle of Veigy, which, although close to the town, was on Bernese territory. His condemnation, however, was to have painful consequences for Calvin.

First, this affair broke his friendship with M. de Falais and his wife. We have seen that this friendship had been very close. The letters which passed between Calvin and these friends show how very intimate they had been. Under the pseudonym of Charles d'Espeville, the Reformer had supported his friends in their departure from their estates and in their wandering life. In 1546, Calvin had dedicated to Jacques de Bourgogne his *Commentary on the First Epistle to the Corinthians*, in terms of great affection and praise. He had drawn up for him in the same year his *Excuse to his Imperial Majesty*. But M. de Falais had been willing to support Bolsec as his doctor. He had, after the imprisonment, written to the Council, 'that the cause of Bolsec's detention was simply that he had spoken to the Congregation freely about doctrine, which ought to be permitted to all Christians without being imprisoned on that account.' This was the occasion of their separation. On the other hand, Calvin learnt that M. de Falais had been in touch with Castellion and had approved his translation of the Bible. The break was thus only the more complete, and not without grief.

When the second edition of the *Commentary on the First Epistle to the Corinthians* appeared in 1556, Calvin dedicated it to Galliaze Caracciole, marquis of Vico, and explained his change of dedication in these terms: 'Would to God that when this commentary first saw the light of day I had not known the man whose name I am now obliged to efface from this page, or at least would to God I had known him better. It is indeed true that I do not fear his being able to accuse me of inconsistency or his complaining that I am taking from him the gift that I had made to him ... but still it is with sorrow that I change my custom and that I have to strike out someone's name from my writings. I am grieved, too, that this man whom I had, as it were, placed in an eminent position by my dedicatory epistle, has moved so far from this position as to be now unable to shine as a good example to others, as was my desire ....'

But the Bolsec affair was to cost Calvin even more than a warm friendship. For in fact after he had left the Château de Veigy, Bolsec, having been expelled from the canton of Berne on Calvin's insistence, went to Paris. In 1562 at the Synod of Orleans he submitted and was reinstated. But, after having been in charge of several parishes in Switzerland and in the Montbéliard region, he returned to the bosom of the Church of Rome. Then, in 1577, he published at Lyons his *History of the Life, Customs, Acts, Doctrines, Constancy and Death of John Calvin, formerly minister at Geneva*. The work was dedicated to the most reverend lord archbishop of the Church at Lyons and primate of France. It is a tissue of injurious lies through which Bolsec pours out his hatred against Calvin whose 'enormous vices' he wishes to describe. He portrays him as a proud, arrogant, cruel, cunning, vindictive and above all, ignorant man. This work formed a kind of arsenal from which Roman Catholic polemical writers, even the great Richelieu, came to draw their ammunition. From this cesspool came the most infamous accusations such as those of sodomy, embezzlement, staging a fake resurrection, greed and lewdness. All these calumnies have been refuted. No historian heeds these falsehoods today. How could a man who, it is maintained, received the

A strange example of Calvin's posthumous fame—
his portrait made up almost entirely of verses of Scripture
(German: 18th century)

criminal brand at Noyon and had to flee his native town because of immoral behaviour—how could he have drawn to Geneva a few years later the civil lieutenant of Noyon, Laurent de Normandie? One may wonder at the fertility of Bolsec's imagination and the persistence of his evil fantasies.

CHAPTER XI

THE SERVETUS DRAMA

ON October 27, 1553, Michael Servetus was burnt after being condemned by the Council of Geneva. The smoke from this fire has never ceased to blacken the memory of Calvin from that day to this. We shall not attempt to dissipate it. In 1903 a committee formed of representatives of the Reformed Churches of Geneva and France set up an expiatory monument on the spot where 350 years previously the stake had stood at Champel. A block of granite bears the name of Michael Servetus and the dates of his birth and his death. On the other face may be read the following inscription: 'Respectful and grateful sons of Calvin, our great Reformer, but condemning an error which belonged to his century and firm believers in the freedom of conscience according to the true principles of the Reformation and the gospel, we have raised this expiatory monument, October 27th, 1903.' There have been not a few criticisms of this monument. Some have said that it was raised more to the glory of Calvin than to the memory of Servetus. However, it must be recognized that such monuments are rare and faults are very rarely recognized with such solemnity.

We must, however, retrace the story of this distressing trial and this lamentable burning, and remove the aura of cruelty with which some have sought to surround the figure of Calvin. Let us say straightway that, though Calvin had Servetus arrested at Geneva and though, during the trial which he had instigated, he was an obstinate accuser and though, for Calvin, the death penalty could be the only possible one for a zealous denier of fundamental doctrines such as the Trinity and infant baptism, he wished, nevertheless, that the punishment by burning should be set aside and be replaced by that of execution. Calvin had no desire to see Servetus at the stake. He wished him to be spared the fire.

But, it will be said, the fact remains. Calvin was intolerant in believing that heretics should be put to death. This is indeed a fault. As we have said earlier, our century institutes no criminal proceedings for heresy, and admits no right of the magistrate to punish offences against the commandments of the first table of the Decalogue. It was not so in the sixteenth century. In 1547, Henri II set in motion in the Parlement of Paris the 'Chambre ardente' which in four years sent to the stake more than six hundred 'Lutherans'. In Switzerland, at Zurich, Constance and Berne during that same period, Anabaptists and anti-Trinitarians such as Servetus were sent to the stake. In the Low Countries, the Inquisition was raging. At Geneva the lonely stake of Servetus is the only object of this kind which provokes disapproval. In other words, such a judgment expects the Reformation to be well in advance of its time. Rilliet wrote: 'The tardy scandal which this punishment caused is homage rendered to the spirit of the Reformation. . . . Anywhere other than in a Reformation town Servetus would have perished without his memory recalling anything more than a stake and a victim. At Geneva he could not lose his life without becoming the representative of a cause and the martyr for a principle.'

Michael Servetus was born at Villeneuve in Aragon on

September 29, 1511. His father was Spanish and his mother French. He had an original mind; in certain respects he was even a genius. He began his studies in law at the age of fourteen. He came to Toulouse, and there became interested in the Bible and the evangelical movement which was beginning in the university with professors like Jean de Caturce who was burned in 1531. At the age of sixteen he became a secretary in the service of a cardinal almoner of Charles V, in whose retinue he crossed France, Italy and Germany. He met Melanchthon at the Diet of Augsburg, Œcolampadius at Basle and Bucer at Strasbourg. His problem at that time was the problem of the Trinity. He denied the Trinitarian doctrine in a little volume in Latin, published at Haguenau in 1531: *De Erroribus Trinitatis (On the Errors of the Trinity)*. For the first time for twelve centuries someone within the bounds of Christendom was taking up the Arian heresy again.

When he was in Paris in 1534, Calvin, who was there at he same time, tried to meet him 'risking', as he said, 'his own life, to win him for our Lord'. But Servetus did not keep the appointment made for the meeting.

About 1540 Servetus, who was at Lyons at that time, wrote to Calvin to put to him three theological questions. They concerned firstly the divinity of Jesus Christ, secondly the kingdom of God and how one enters it, and thirdly baptism. 'To wit, whether baptism should take place in faith, like the Supper and to what end both are instituted in the New Testament.' Calvin replied to him in detail on these three questions.

In 1553 Servetus wrote his *Christianismi Restitutio*, a collection of several treatises in which he sets forth his doctrine; in it pantheistic elements are clearly discernible. During the course of one of his expositions on redemption by blood, he sets out his discovery of the lesser circulation of the blood (pulmonary circulation), of which he was thus aware three-quarters of a century before Harvey. In his writings he made no secret of his intention to fight against Calvin's doctrine. The title of his book makes this clear. After *Christianae Religionis Institutio*, here comes *Christianismi Restitutio*; after the 'institution', the 'restitution'. He denied the Trinity. Yet his book contained formulae which would seem to many to be quite orthodox. 'Christ is God, truly God, substantially God, for the deity is in Him bodily.' However, these affirmations must be interpreted in the sense of a communication by God of His substance, first to the Son of God, then to the apostles, then to believers. He makes the matter clearer in these words: 'All things are a part and portion of God and all nature is His substantial spirit.'

In the same volume following the *Restitutio*, Servetus, who had only signed his initials, M.S.V., published thirty-two letters which he had written to Calvin to refute the doctrines of the *Institutes*. These letters had been transmitted to Calvin by a bookseller of Lyons, Jean Frelon. They had no confidential character since Servetus then published them. Calvin thanked Jean Frelon for his parcel in these terms:

'Seigneur Jean, because your most recent letters were brought to me at the moment I was leaving, I had no leisure to reply to what was therein enclosed. Since my return at the first moment of leisure that I had, I was very happy to satisfy your desire. Not that I have any great hope of being any use towards such a man, from what I can see of the way he is set; but I will make the attempt to see whether there might be any means of bringing him back to the truth, which will only happen if God works in him so that he becomes another person. Because he had written to me in so proud a spirit I was very desirous of quelling his pride a little, speaking more harshly than my custom. But I could do no other, for I assure you that there is no lesson which is more necessary for him to learn than humility. And this will come to him from the Spirit of God and from nowhere else. But we must also set our hands to this task. If God gives us grace in this matter, grace to him and grace to us, and if the present reply is profitable to him, I shall certainly have cause to rejoice. If he goes on in a style like that which he adopts at the moment, you will be wasting your time in asking me to do any more work for him, for I have other matters which press me more urgently. I should make it a matter of conscience to be still busy about such matters, not doubting that it [the Servetus controversy] was a device of Satan to distract me from other more useful reading.'

In writing to Calvin Servetus had said that he would willingly go to Geneva to finish off the task of convincing him. Calvin spoke of this to Farel in a letter in which he let fall this terrible harsh remark: 'I will not pledge my word to him [for his coming to Geneva] for if he came I should not, wielding what little influence I have, allow him to depart alive.' There we are—a premeditated plot, a plan already afoot, it has been said. Not at all, but certainly a harsh attitude in the battle for doctrine in which Calvin was engaged, and in which, let us say again, to deny a fundamental truth like the Trinity seemed to him a crime greater than any crime towards society and consequently more worthy of punishment. And besides, this was the opinion of all the men of the times, apart from Castellion. Speaking of Servetus, Bolsec himself said: 'I do not write these things out of pleasure for the death of such a monstrous heretic, for he was evil and unworthy to live amongst men, and I would like all similar men to be exterminated and the Church well purged of such vermin.'

Moreover, Servetus had no illusions about the matter. He wrote to Abel Poupin, one of the pastors at Geneva, 'I know without a doubt that I shall have to die for this cause, but for all that I do not lose courage, so that I may become a disciple like my Master.'

But we must now say something of the course of this trial. Let us first give Voltaire's version which has been the source of numerous accusations, since amplified and envenomed.

'Calvin and Servetus disputed by letter. From disputation Calvin passed to insult and from insult to this theological hatred which is the most implacable of all hatreds. By some deception Calvin had obtained the pages of a work that Servetus was secretly having printed. He sent them to Lyons with letters which he had received from him, an action which would be enough to dishonour him forever in society, for what is called the spirit of society is the most honest and severe of all synods. Calvin had Servetus accused by an emissary: what a part for an apostle to play! Servetus, who knew that in France any innovator was burnt without mercy, fled whilst the trial against him was in progress. Unfortunately he had to go through Geneva. Calvin got to know of it and denounced him. . . . When his enemy was in prison he heaped injuries and ill-treatment upon him, as cowards do when they are masters. By dint of exerting pressure on the judges, and using the influence of those under his leadership, and by shouting and getting others to shout, that God demanded the execution of Michael Servetus, he had him burnt alive and enjoyed his torment. Such was the work of Calvin, the very man who would have been burnt himself if he had set one foot in France, the man who had raised his voice so loudly against all persecution.'

We desired to quote this page to show that there is also an anti-theological hatred. In actual fact in all that Voltaire says there is not one word of truth.

For a start, Calvin did not receive a copy of *Christianismi Restitutio* as a result of any deception. He received it direct and in the normal way from the bookseller, Jean Frelon. It is supposed that this copy sent to Calvin is one of the rarest copies still extant and it is to be found in the *Bibliothèque nationale* in Paris. Colladon, one of Calvin's secretaries, made an index to it which he wrote himself on the last pages. There is nothing deceitful about that.

Then again, Calvin did not have Servetus denounced by an emissary to the Roman Inquisition. Here are the facts. There was in Geneva in 1553 a French refugee who was very devoted to Calvin named Guillaume de Trie. The latter still corresponded with his cousin at Lyons, Antoine Arney, who had remained a fervent Roman Catholic. In a letter, Arney had reproached de Trie for having embraced Reformation ideas and having entered a Church which had no order or discipline, for the Reformers 'have introduced a licence to sow confusion everywhere'. Cut to the quick, de Trie replied that whilst at Lyons the Roman Church was cruelly burning men who called on the name of Jesus Christ (alluding to the five students who were tortured there), they allowed a blasphemer who denied the Trinity and destroyed the foundations of faith and condemned infant baptism as an invention of the devil, to live in peace. And he went on: 'the man of whom I speak has been condemned in all these Churches that you reproach. However, amongst you he is allowed even to have his books printed which are so full of blasphemies that I must not say any more about them. He is a Portuguese Spaniard whose real name is Michael Servetus, but he calls himself Villeneuve at the moment, pretending to be a doctor. He has been sometime at Lyons. Now he is staying in Vienne, where the book I mentioned was printed by a certain fellow who set up his printing press there, Balthazar Arnoullet. So that you don't think I am speaking from hearsay, I am sending you the first page as a proof.'

So there was denunciation; but it was the doing of Guillaume de Trie and not of Calvin. The French refugee did this when provoked by accusations of licence hurled by Arney, and in grief over the martyrdom of the five students at Lyons.

Antoine Arney might have kept this denunciation to himself. He decided otherwise and reported the fact to the Inquisitor of Lyons, Matthieu Ory. The latter set an enquiry on foot. Servetus was questioned at Vienne. He was shown the first page of his book. He denied that he was the author of it and the printer denied it too. The Inquisitor then declared to Arney that the proofs were insufficient and that fuller information would be needed before any action could be taken. Arney then wrote to de Trie, who replied in these terms.

'Sir cousin, when I wrote that letter to you which you have sent to those who in it were charged with negligence, I had no thought that the thing would go so far. My intention was simply to prove to you what fine zeal and devotion was theirs who call themselves pillars of the Church yet allow such disorder in their midst, while on the other hand, they persecute so harshly poor Christians who are only desirous of following God in simplicity. Because the example was so notable and I had been informed of it, it seemed that an opportunity was offered to mention it in my letters as bearing on the matter in hand. But since you have made public what I had intended for your private ear alone, God grant that it may be for the best in purging Christendom of such filth. If they have so keen a desire to deal with the matter as you say, it seems that the thing should not be too difficult, although I can't at the moment furnish you with what you demand, i.e. the printed book. I shall hand over to you more material to convict him, to wit, two dozen tracts written by the man in question in which part of his heresies is contained. If you were to put before him the printed book he could deny it, which he will not be able to do with his own hand-writing.... But I must admit one thing: I had great difficulty in getting what I am sending you out of M. Calvin. Not that he does not wish such execrable blasphemies to be repressed, but because it seems to him that his own duty as far as he is concerned, having no sword of justice, is to convince heretics by teaching rather than pursuing them by this means. But I have bothered him so much, showing him how I might be reproached with frivolous levity if he did not help me, that in the end he decided to give me them.'

This letter is of great importance. It shows first that de Trie did not think that his cousin would hand the matter over to the Inquisition, but since the matter had been embarked upon and he was accused of false witness, he would go through with it. He asked Calvin to hand over the personal letters which Servetus had sent him. Calvin at first refused, for he wished to convince Servetus, not to punish him. He was a theologian and not a magistrate. He did not hold the sword of justice, he was not the dictator of Geneva and his principal desire was that this denier should be brought back to the truth. But he gave in in order not to put de Trie in a false position and handed over the originals of the letters which Servetus published at the end of his *Restitutio*. This was a mistake. But is this 'the action which would suffice to dishonour him for ever in society' that Voltaire speaks of? We doubt it.

Moreover, Calvin defended himself in advance from such accusations. 'The rumour is flying around that I engineered the taking of Servetus in a popish land, that is at Vienne. Whereupon several people say that I did not behave honestly by exposing him to the mortal enemies of the faith, as if I had thrown him into the jaws of the wolves. But I beg you, how should I have suddenly become on such familiar terms with the satellites of the pope? A most credible thing indeed that we should write to each other, and that those who agree with me as well as Belial does with Jesus Christ, should plot with so mortal an enemy, just as they would with their own bosom friends! That is why there is no need to insist at any greater length in order to refute so baseless a calumny, which falls to the ground if I say simply in one word that there is nothing to it.'

We may trust Calvin when he says 'there is nothing to it'. He had no intention of providing the Inquisition with weapons, but only of supporting the statements of a friend.

Once armed with these letters, the Inquisitor Ory had Servetus and Arnoullet arrested on April 5, 1553. Servetus was questioned, particularly on the two pages of the *Institutes* which were covered with his annotations. This reminds us of a statement of Calvin's, 'he hurls himself on all my books that he can get hold of, loading every margin with insults like a dog who had bitten or gnawed away at some stone.' These Inquisitors who used annotations to the *Institutes* in order to judge an accused man were strange people. Servetus retracted on all counts contained in the accusation but the next day he escaped from prison. He was then condemned in his absence to the punishment of the stake, and burned in effigy with five bundles of his book.

After his escape Servetus wandered for four months in various districts. Then he went to Geneva. Some say that he did not wish to stop there but was making only a temporary halt there on his way to Piémont. Others believe that, knowing of Calvin's critical position in only having a narrow majority for him in the Councils, Servetus wished to defy him even in his own city. On Sunday, August 13, he went to the Church of the Madeleine to hear Calvin preach. He was recognized amongst the congregation by some of the faithful, denounced to the criminal lieutenant and arrested. A complaint was lodged against him by Calvin's secretary, Nicolas de la Fontaine who, in accordance with the Genevan law, was imprisoned at the same time as the man he had accused. The trial lasted from August 15 to 17. It was a painful business in which Calvin discussed with Servetus the authority of Scripture and his anti-Trinitarian and pantheistic doctrines. Servetus defended himself skilfully and found a certain amount of support from Calvin's enemies at Geneva, men like Philibert Berthelier. In its uncertainty the Council decided to ask the opinion of other Swiss cities, Berne, Basle, Zurich and Schaffhausen, and to ask Vienne to convey to them the records of the trial. On September 1, a discussion took place before the judges between Servetus and Calvin, but it was not a public discussion, for the magistrate did not wish to let go of his authority in favour of that of the people; it was a discussion in Latin on various texts.

The trial dragged on. Servetus suffered in his cell from tattered clothes covered with vermin. He wrote to the Council: 'You see that Calvin is at the end of his tether, he does not know what to say. For his own enjoyment he wishes to see me perish here in prison. The fleas are eating me alive. My breeches are torn and I have no change of clothing, neither doublet nor shirt, apart from one poor one. I demand that my cause should be placed before the Council of the Two Hundred with my requests.' The Council had a change of clothes sent to him. On September 22, his tone becomes more peremptory. 'Gentlemen, I demand that my false accuser [Calvin] be punished with the punishment of the *lex talionis* and be detained prisoner as I am myself until the case be finished by the death of one or other of us, or some other punishment. And for this purpose I formally indict him with the said punishment of the *lex talionis*. I am content to die if he is not convicted, either of this or of other things which I shall bring against him ... Magician that he is, he must not only be condemned but he must be exterminated, hounded from your city, and his goods must be adjudged to me as a recompence for mine which he has caused me to lose.'

On October 18, the reply from the Swiss churches arrived. They all decided that Servetus was guilty. They had not to pronounce on his punishment, which was the business of the Genevan magistrates, but their opinion was clear. In a private comment, Haller of Berne, giving his account of the session, said of his colleagues: 'They all shuddered with indignation to such an extent that I had no doubt that if he were in their hands he would be delivered to the flames. They added to our reply a letter in which they exhort the Genevans to root out this pestilence for fear that the neighbouring fields be damaged by their negligence.'

This reply from the Swiss cities made the nature of the Geneva Council's decision certain. On October 26, despite the attempt of Calvin's enemies, for example Ami Perrin, the Council decided that Servetus should be condemned to be taken to Champel and there burned alive and his books burnt. Immediately the sentence was known,

Calvin wrote to Farel: 'Tomorrow Servetus will be taken to his punishment. We have done everything we can to change the type of death, but in vain.' On which Rilliet commented thus: 'Legal custom, which had already been followed by the judge of Vienne, won the day over Calvin's request. Yet he is the one who is always held responsible for the burning which he desired should never take place.'

One last interview took place between the two men before the ordeal. Servetus asked Calvin to forgive him. The latter replied: 'I profess that I never held any personal grievance against you. You must remember that more than sixteen years ago when I was at Paris I spared no effort to win you for our Lord. If you had yielded to reason I might have been used to reconcile you with all God's faithful servants. You avoided the struggle then, yet I never ceased to exhort you by letter. But all has been useless. You hurled yourself against me in incredible rage rather than mere anger. For the rest, as far as my person is concerned, I will say no more. Think rather of beseeching God for His forgiveness, the God whom you have blasphemed by wishing to efface the three Persons who are in His essence. Rather ask the Son of God for His pardon, the one whom you have disfigured and virtually denied as Saviour.'

Then Servetus went to his punishment, accompanied by Farel. As he died he said, 'Eternal Son of God, have pity on me.'

Yes, this dramatic burning of Servetus is a terrible thing. Life is sacred, and no one man has the right to condemn another to death. Castellion spoke truly when, a short time after the burning, he said: 'To kill a man is not to protect a doctrine, it is to kill a man.' Having said that, can we attempt to assess the gravity of this struggle and to estimate its consequences? If Servetus had triumphed, Calvin's authority in his reforming work at Geneva would have been compromised. When the outcome of the trial seemed uncertain, he thought of leaving and Bullinger wrote to him: 'Walther's account left me sad and uneasy. Do not abandon, I beseech you, a Church which contains so many excellent men. Bear all things for the cause of the elect. Stay then. . . . The Lord will not leave you.' For one moment the opportunity seemed to favour the free-thinkers in their desire to shake off an authority which they found too heavy. The general opinion of the other Swiss towns prevented this reversal. Calvin brings this out during the course of the trial, despite the invective employed which makes him very much a man of the sixteenth century. The truth of God has been attacked. The Trinity is openly denied. The authority of the Bible is called in question. The very foundations of the faith are put into the melting-pot. Calvin is staggered by such denials and by such blasphemy. Our own century, a faithless century caring little for doctrine, is astounded at this firmness and calls it harshness. Calvin was wrong to think that heresy was to be punished by banishment and death, but he was right to think that the denial of the Trinity and the divinity of Christ were infinitely serious matters and constituted an attack on the gospel of salvation and on the work of the whole Reformation movement.

Protests arose on all sides. In 1554 Calvin wrote in Latin his *Défense contre la Foi orthodoxe sur la Sainte Trinité*, against the detestable errors of Servetus. This work provoked from Sébastien Castellion, under the pseudonym of Martin Bellie, the treatise *On Heretics*, debating whether they should be proceeded against. It was a collection of short extracts from Luther, Brenz, Erasmus, Lactantius, Calvin himself, Augustine, Chrysostom, Jerome, and Castellion, showing that the heretics cannot be punished and that force cannot be exercised in the domain of faith. 'The sword cannot reach the soul.' By this book Castellion became a precursor of toleration. He was ahead of his time. May we, however, affirm in opposition to those who have seen fit to oppose Castellion to Calvin, that Castellion has not the same responsibilities of directing the Church as Calvin had, nor the same struggles to undergo? Castellion was right to condemn the terrible custom of punishing heretics by burning but, on the other hand, Calvin considered that the greatest danger that the Reformation could encounter in its early years was the denial of the Christian doctrine of the Trinity and the authority of Holy Scripture. And he, too, was right.

CHAPTER XII

CALVIN'S LAST YEARS

THE trial of Servetus marked not only the tensest moment of the struggle in which Calvin was engaged at Geneva against the 'libertins'[1], but also the moment of their defeat. Despite their opposition to the Reformer, these men had seen that they could not run a successful opposition movement against the united front of the other cities. The most fiery of them, five in number, stayed away when the vote was taken, and the twenty Councillors who were in session, although not all Calvin's supporters, condemned Servetus. A short time afterwards, Berthelier took up his old pretensions on the basis of the city Council's right to raise a decree of excommunication pronounced by the Consistory and thus to place a Church decision under the control of the magistrates. Here again, the Council decided to ask the opinion of the other Swiss cities, Berne, Zurich, Basle and Schaffhausen; with the exception of Berne, they declared in favour of Calvin. The years went by. A new generation trained in the principles of the Reformation was gradually coming to power and numerous French refugees who were all favourable to Calvin exerted their influence too. In 1555 the scales turned and the majority in the Councils secured the appointment of friends of Calvin as the four

---

[1] This was the name given to those who found the effects of Calvin's ascendancy at Geneva too strict. Their morals are not in question, as the present sense of the word might imply.

elected syndics. There were some commotions in the street, a few blows were exchanged, but the 'libertins' had lost the game.

This respite allowed Calvin to devote himself to a work which was in a way to crown his ministry at Geneva, the foundation of the Academy in 1559. Here again, we must underline the inspiration gained at Strasbourg during his stay from 1538 to 1540. He had come into contact with the college founded by John Sturm and had taught there. On his return to Geneva he had given a large place to the organization of education in the Articles of 1541. But despite the presence of the great pedagogue, Maturin Cordier, until 1545, this educational programme was not easily realized. Sébastien Castellion was its moving spirit for some time but he left Geneva in 1544 for Basle. However, in 1559 a dispute between the professors at Lausanne and the Bernese government on the evergreen question of the right of excommunication pronounced by the Consistory apart from the civil law, brought about the departure of several professors from the Lausanne school. They came to Geneva. Amongst them was Theodore Beza, who was nominated Professor of Greek at the college, and first Rector of the Academy; he rapidly became Calvin's right-hand man. There was also Pierre Viret, François Bérauld, Jean Tagault and Antoine Chevalier. These men formed the brilliant team of teachers. Their arrival permitted the foundation of the Geneva Academy on June 15, 1559. The teaching of the Academy was given in two cycles: the cycle of the *Schola privata*, which corresponded to our secondary education and comprised the teaching of French, Latin, Greek and philosophy, and that of the *Schola publica* which was a university education, teaching Hebrew, Greek, the Arts, i.e. philosophy and literature, and above all, theology.

By the foundation of this Academy Calvin began to make Geneva the intellectual centre of the French-speaking Reformation. Students flocked from all parts. This was the moment when, after several years of intense gospel preaching by courageous colporteurs, the churches were 'set up' in France and were organized according to the Calvinist model, a Council of presbyters electing its

The College—the Main Steps

pastor. The first to be thus organized in that country was the Church of Paris in 1555. Because of the persecution which was raging violently at that time due to the work of the 'Chambre ardente', this Church was from the beginning constituted apart from the State. It elected its elders and its pastors without intervention or domination from the civil power. It had thus from the very first what neither the German nor even the Genevan Reformation had been able to attain, the liberty of the Church, its independence *vis-à-vis* the prince or the magistrate. Instead of being nominated by the town Councils as at Geneva and Strasbourg, the elders of the first church in France were elected by the assembly of believers. The progress of these churches was to be rapid. In 1555 there was one church; in 1559 there were thirty churches sending delegates to the first national synod at Paris. In 1561 there were 2,150 churches, if we may trust the list presented by Coligny to Catherine de Medici. Pastors were needed for all these parishes. They were trained at Geneva and attended Calvin's lectures in the auditorium in great crowds. And Calvin wrote: 'Send us wood and we will send you back arrows.'

The Rector's book of the names of these students from 1559 contains the names of people from all districts of France and from several European countries. We find there the name Olevianus, one of the authors of the Heidelberg Catechism, that admirable exposition of the Reformed faith; that of Marnix de Sainte-Aldegonde, one of the leaders in the Low Countries; that of Thomas Bodley, future founder of the famous Bodleian Library at Oxford; of Lambert Daneau, one of the fine second-generation Calvinist theologians. Amongst those who sat at Calvin's feet the most celebrated was doubtless John Knox, the Scottish Reformer. In 1554 he was an enthusiastic listener to the great theologian and later applied in his own country the principles of faith and discipline which he had learnt at Geneva.[1]

The teaching of Calvin was essentially biblical. His lectures were published in the form of commentaries. Sometimes, as in those on the Minor Prophets, we have even preserved for us the prayers with which he would

[1] *Translator's note.* For a popular account of Knox's work see A. M. Renwick, *The Story of the Scottish Reformation*, 1960.

begin and finish his lecture. Here is one of them: 'May the Lord God grant to us to deal with the mysteries of His heavenly wisdom in such a way that we may truly profit in the fear of His holy Name to His glory and to our edification. Amen.' Calvin used to lecture and preach extempore but he had secretaries present who took down his words at great speed and thus permitted them to be published. Here is how this was done.

'As it might be considered strange, nay, even quite incredible that these lectures were recorded, and with such diligence that John Calvin never said a single word while expounding which was not straightway set down, it will be good to inform our readers briefly at this point of the means employed by those who recorded them. For once their zeal and remarkable industry have been made known, this may occasion several others to undertake a similar work and thus the thing will not seem incredible.

'Firstly, you must understand that the said Calvin never wrote down or noted anything for his public exposition of Holy Scripture, and still less when he had finished his lecture, or the day after he had taught; but for the space of an hour he continually expounded, without however taking down a single word in his book in order that he might remember it. This was why Jean Budé and Claude de Jonviller, having found some years previously that the trouble they had taken to record the lectures on the Psalms had not been useless, were the more encouraged to record with greater diligence, if that were possible, all the lectures on the twelve Minor Prophets. Moreover the means that they adopt to take down the lectures is that each of them has his paper ready as conveniently as possible and each writes separately as quickly as he can. If one fails to catch any particular word, as sometimes happens, especially when Calvin becomes vehement as he expounds some passages which demand this, the other may have recorded it, or the author can easily put the word in. For as soon as the lecture is over, the said Jonviller takes away the papers of the two others and collates them with his. He carefully looks over them and diligently compares them. Then he has another person transcribe what has been recorded so hastily. Finally he looks over the whole thing, so that the next day he may read it over to the author at his own home. Where there is sometimes a word lacking, he can restore it. Or if there is something which does not seem to be expounded clearly enough he can explain more simply. That is how these lectures came to be published. . . .'[1]

Thanks to these rapid notes by his secretaries, the commentaries that Calvin produced on all the books of the Bible except the Song of Songs and Revelation have been published. Let us give here some of the dates of these editions of his commentaries. Romans: 1540; Corinthians: 1546 and 1547; Galatians, Ephesians, Philippians, Colossians, 1 and 2 Timothy: 1548; Titus and Hebrews: 1549; 1 and 2 Thessalonians and James: 1550; 1 and 2 Peter and Jude: 1551; Acts of the Apostles and Isaiah: 1552; St. John's Gospel: 1553; Genesis: 1554; Harmony of the Gospels: 1555; Psalms: 1557; Minor Prophets: 1559–60; Daniel: 1561; the Pentateuch and Jeremiah: 1563; Joshua: 1564. The preface of this last commentary on Joshua, which appeared after Calvin's death, was devoted by Theodore Beza to the narrative of Calvin's life, and was thus the first of the Reformer's biographies. Through his commentaries which retain their value over the centuries in view of their spiritual wealth, Calvin deserves the title of 'prince of exegetes'. Their theological impor-

---

[1] From the Printer's Foreword to Calvin's *Lectures on the Minor Prophets* (Geneva, 1560).

tance is very great, since we have been able to reconstruct Calvin's doctrine of salvation from his commentaries, even apart from the *Institutes*.

Besides his lectures and daily preaching, Calvin kept up an extremely important correspondence with a large number of people. The editors of the *Opera Calvini* dedicated eleven volumes of their collection to the publication of these letters. These volumes contain 4,271 letters addressed to 307 different persons or groups. There are letters to friends, such as those written to Farel, to Viret, to Bucer, to Beza; there are letters of spiritual counsel and others dealing with matters of ecclesiastical government. The letters addressed to churches, sometimes the humblest, are numerous. Calvin as a veritable messenger of God knew how to speak firmly to the great ones of this world without fear or servility, as may be seen from his letters to Marguerite d'Angoulême, to Renée of Ferrara, to the King of Navarre, Antoine de Bourbon and his wife Jeanne d'Albret, to the young King of England, Edward VI, to the English Protector, the Duke of Somerset, to the Elector Palatine, Frederick III, who asked the two theologians, Olevianus and Ursinus to draw up the Heidelberg Catechism which was adopted by the Synod of the Palatinate in 1563.

By means of this correspondence Calvin's activity extended far beyond the walls of Geneva and spread throughout Europe. First it spread to France, in which country he was in continual contact with the churches. At the first national synod of Paris in 1559, he sent a plan for a Confession of Faith of which only the first articles were re-worded and which has become the Confession of Faith for the Reformed Churches of France. It should be called the Paris Confession of Faith, though it bears the name of The Confession of Faith of La Rochelle, for it was in the course of a synod held there in 1571 that it was solemnly adopted by three national Churches, the Reformed Church of Béarn, represented by Jeanne d'Albret, the Reformed Church of Geneva, represented by Theodore Beza and the Reformed Church of France represented principally by Antoine de Chandieu. Calvin did not take part in the Colloquy of Poissy (1561), for the Smaller Council at Geneva would not allow him to venture into France, but he closely followed its debates led in such masterly fashion by Theodore Beza, who sent him a daily account of what was taking place.

In Belgium Calvin's influence can be seen on Guy de Brès, the author of the Confession of Faith of the Low Countries in 1561. The Belgian Reformer had stayed at Geneva in 1556 and had followed Calvin's lectures there. That same year John Knox, the Scottish Reformer, wrote to a friend: 'I have no fear at all of saying that Geneva is the most perfect school of Christ that has ever been on the earth since the time of the apostles. Elsewhere, I grant, Christ is preached in all truth, but I know no town in which religion and morals are so thoroughly reformed.'

When he was invited to go to Poland in 1557, Calvin had to decline the invitation for health reasons, but by his letters he exerted a profound influence on the nobility of the country and Reformation doctrine was widespread there. From 1556 to 1560 the Calvinist Church of Poland was led by Jean a Lasco, who had been formerly the Reformer of La Frise, at Emden, and had also been in England. Unfortunately, Poland was also influenced by the Socinians, Faustus Socinus and Blandrata. Ten years after the death of Calvin, these two went and settled in Poland and founded an anti-Trinitarian church at Cracow. Their writings have been collected in the six great

volumes which form the library of the brothers of Poland.
By its unitarian doctrines this Church was to bring about
the ruin of Calvinism in Poland.

In Hungary the Reformer Devay, favouring Lutheran
doctrines at first, sided with the principles of the *Institutes*,
hence the Hungarian Reformation became Calvinist for
the most part. Calvin had connections by letter with
Hungary and Hungarian students came to Geneva. Their
confession, which has a clearly Calvinist emphasis, is the
work of the Reformer, Melius of Debrecen.

Thus by lectures, preaching and letters and the successive editions of the *Institutes* and the treatises, a veritably
European enterprise was set up with its centre at Geneva.

Calvin was a man whose outlook was European and at
the same time ecumenical. He had the vision of the
Churches of the Reformation united, and their separation
pained him. We have mentioned above how he began a
movement of union by signing with Bullinger the agreement on the sacraments (*Consensus Tigurinus*). One phrase
of this consensus raised the Lutheran theologians against
him and was the cause of a long controversy with Joachim
Westphal and Tileman Heshus. But for all that Calvin
never lost his ecumenical vision. In 1552 the primate of
England, Thomas Cranmer, wrote to him from Lambeth
to ask, as he did also to Melanchthon and Bullinger,
whether they might not be able to establish a common
doctrine of the sacraments. Calvin replied to him shortly
afterwards and from his letter we shall quote these lines:
'Doubtless it must be counted among the greatest mis-
fortunes of our century that the Churches are thus
separated from each other so that scarcely one human link
remains between us, and that the holy communion of the
members of Christ which many confess with their mouth
is only sincerely sought after by few. . . . From this it

follows that the members being so scattered, the body of the Church lies bleeding (*Ita fit ut, membris dissipatis, lacerum jaceat ecclesiae corpus*). This affects me so deeply that if anybody could see that I might be of any use I should not hesitate to cross ten seas for this business, if that were needful. . . . Indeed, if learned men were to seek a solid and carefully devised agreement according to the rule of Scripture, an agreement by which the separated Churches should unite with each other, I think that for my part I ought not to spare any trouble or dangers.'[1] Despite his desire, this unity of the Church was not, alas, on the point of being realized.

Now this immense labour was accomplished under the burden of continual illness by a man who suffered much, and whom death was to take at the age of fifty-five in 1564. His health had been ruined in his college years by bad food and intensity of study. But in 1558–59 his illness got worse though he did relax his labours as a writer on this account. In a letter of February, 1564, he gives a detailed description of the symptoms of his illness to the doctors of Montpellier, who at that time were in favour of the Reformation. It was then that he gave his last lecture to the Academy and preached his last sermon. On April 28, he said farewell to the pastors of Geneva in terms of moving humility. Going over his memories at his last hour, he told them among other things:

'. . . When I first came to this Church there was, as it were, nothing. There was preaching and that was all. They sought out idols and burnt them, but there was no Reformation. Everything was in confusion. There was good old master Guillaume [Farel] and blind Coraud, who was not born blind, but he became blind at Basle.

[1] *Op. Calv.*, XIV, pp. 312–314.

There was also master Antoine Saunier and that fine preacher Froment who used to leave his shop and go into the pulpit and then go back to his shop, where he continued chatting and thus preached a double sermon.

'My life here has been spent in strange conflicts. In the evening at my own front door I have been greeted with derision by fifty or sixty blunderbuss shots. Can you imagine how that would astonish a poor, timid scholar such as I am, and have always been, I readily confess. Then, after I was thrown out of the town, I went to Strasbourg, where having stayed some time, I was recalled. But I did not have any less difficulty than previously when I wished to take over my responsibility. They set the dogs at my tail, crying "Knave! Knave!" and they took me by the legs and by the gown. I went to the Council of the Two Hundred when they were fighting and I held back the others who wanted to go there but who were not built for that sort of work. . . . And when I went in they said to me, "Sir, withdraw; it's not you that we are aiming at." I said to them, "I shall not do so. Come now, evildoers, kill me and my blood will rise against you, these very benches will require it of you." Thus I have been in the midst of many a struggle and you shall undergo others which shall be no less, but even greater. For you are a perverse and unhappy nation, and although there are people of goodwill among you, the nation is perverse and evil. You will have much to do when God has taken me. For although I am nothing, I know that I have prevented three thousand tumults which might have taken place in Geneva. But take courage and strengthen yourselves, for God will use this church and will maintain it; I assure you that God will keep it.

'I have had much infirmity with which you have had to bear, and even the total of all I have done has been worth nothing. Evil men will take this word up, but I still say that all that I have done has been worth nothing, and that I am a miserable creature. But I can say that I desired your good, that my vices have always displeased me and the root of the fear of God was in my heart. . . .

'As to my doctrine I have taught faithfully and God has granted me the grace of being able to write, which I have done as faithfully as I have been able, and I have not corrupted one single passage of Scripture nor twisted it as far as I know, and when I might well have brought in subtle meanings, if I had studied subtlety, I have trampled the whole lot underfoot, and I have always studied to be simple. I have written nothing out of hatred against anyone but I have always set before me faithfully what I considered was for the glory of God. . . .

'On my return from Strasbourg I drew up the Catechism in haste, for I would never have wished to accept the ministry unless they had sworn to be faithful on these two matters, to wit, to keep the Catechism and discipline; and as I wrote it they came and got the pieces of paper as broad as your hand and took them to the printing-press. Although master Pierre Viret was in the town, do you think that I ever showed him anything of it? I never had the leisure to; I had sometimes thought that I might set my hand to the task if I had the leisure.

'As to the Sunday prayers, I took the Strasbourg form, and borrowed the greater part of it. Of the others I could not take them from there, for not a word of them existed, but I took them all from Scripture.

'I was also constrained to draw up the form of the baptismal service when I was at Strasbourg and when they brought me Anabaptist children from five or ten leagues around, to baptize them. It was a rough service that I drew up but I advise you not to change it.'

A few days later his old friend and fellow warrior, Farel, came from Neuchâtel to see him. Calvin breathed his last on May 27, 1564, at the setting of the sun. He was buried very simply in the cemetery of Plainpalais. No stone marks his grave. Thus died without glory the man who throughout his life had proclaimed that to God alone belongs all the glory.

CHAPTER XIII

CALVIN'S PIETY

THIS chapter is no study of Calvin's theology, for we consider it sufficient to have given a survey of Calvin's thought and method—which is essentially biblical—in our earlier pages on the questions of election and the Lord's Supper. An analysis of the *Institutes* would take up too much space within the limits that we have set ourselves. We believe it would be more useful to say a few words about Calvin's piety.

The revolution which Calvin initiated in the domain of piety has been compared to that which Copernicus brought about in the realm of cosmology in the same period. Before Copernicus it was held that the sun revolved around the earth, which was considered as the centre of the universe. In his celebrated book on the *Revolution of the Celestial Orbs*, the learned astronomer proved that, on the contrary, it was the earth that revolved around the sun. Hence the whole conception of the cosmos was changed. Similarly, Calvin removed the usual centre of piety which was the soul of man, its needs and its outpourings and restored to piety its true centre—God. Religion consists in worshipping God and serving Him. Even in his 1542 Catechism, Calvin had declared:

'God created us and set us in the world to be glorified in us. It is very reasonable, since He is the author and principle of our life, that we should give back to Him all His glory.'

Others had said it before him, but he said it with a power and with an obstinacy which put back this too-easily-forgotten principle of God's glory into the first place. Since he had himself powerfully felt this grip of God on his life at the time of his conversion, and at the decisive stages in his ministry, Calvin affirmed the sovereign grace which saves a life to train it in service and in obedience towards the Lord. The soul, freed from preoccupation with itself, delivered from self-scrutiny and vain analyses, forgets itself and denies itself in order to think solely of God and His work.

I am thinking of the man who said to me a short time ago as he came out of a lecture, 'I have just been converted through reading the *Institutes*.' And when I asked him to tell me what exactly had been the message which had effected this transformation in his life, he replied: 'I learnt from reading Calvin that all the worries about health and about the uncertain future which had hitherto dominated my life were without much importance and that the only things that counted were obedience to the will of God and a care for His glory.' Never let it be said that Calvinist thinking is remote from our twentieth-century way of looking at things and that Calvin no longer has anything to say to the men of our time.

God's sovereignty over every moment of life is clearly opposed to the secularization which is the hallmark of our time. Little by little the whole of our existence has been split off from its deepest roots in God. Religion appears now as a private affair, unconnected with public life. But it is precisely this secularization which must force the Christian of our time to re-affirm the glory of God in a world which fails to recognize Him. In the sixteenth century Calvin's thought was certainly always found in a clearly defined context of opposition and persecution. It

IOANNES CALVINUS NATUS NOVIODUNI PICARDORUM

is a doctrine for men in prison, for the tortured, for the witnesses who are beheaded. But it is just as necessary in the dramatic situation of the twentieth century where there are also prisons, tortures and executions for those who confess Christ in certain countries, and where there is also a desire to push God out of human life. For God will not yield His glory to another.

The stress that Calvin laid on the sovereignty of God must never make us think, however, that he left on one side the importance of a relationship with Jesus Christ. Jesus said: 'Believe in God, believe also in me' (John xiv. 1). Like all true Christian doctrine, the Reformer's thought is Trinitarian. He quotes the saying of Gregory of Nazianzus: 'I cannot conceive of the One without the Three shining around me' (*Institutes*, I, xiii, 17). We might describe this theology not only as 'theocentric' but also as 'christocentric'. We could also show, with one of his modern commentators[1], the primary place that the Holy Spirit holds in this theology.

But it is the place of Christ in Calvinistic piety that we would especially underline here. 'We cannot move the smallest distance from Jesus Christ without our salvation vanishing away, since it resides entirely in Him. All those who do not rest and delight in Him forfeit all grace' (*Institutes*, II, xvi, 1). And later: 'We have no full and sound conjunction with Him unless Jesus Christ joins us to Him, and indeed if we would have the assurance that God loves us and is favourably disposed towards us, we must cast our eyes on Jesus Christ and remain in Him' (*Institutes*, II, xvi, 3). Book III of the *Institutes* sets forth the manner of participating in the grace of Jesus Christ, the fruits which result from this and the blessings which follow. Here is the beginning of this book: 'We have now

[1] Charles Lelièvre: *La Maîtrise de L'Esprit*.

to see how the riches that God the Father has set in His
Son come to us. . . . As long as we are outside of Christ
and separated from Him, all that He has done or suffered
for the salvation of the human race is useless and of no
importance. In order to communicate to us the blessings
with which the Father has filled and enriched Him, it is
therefore needful that He should be made ours, that He
should dwell in us. . . . Nothing of what He possesses
belongs to us until we are made one with Him' (III, i, 1).

This union with Christ is the work of the Holy Spirit,
and this work of the Holy Spirit has another name, it is
called faith. Calvin gives this admirable definition of
faith: 'Faith embraces Jesus Christ' (III, ii, 8). Few
theologians have had a more living and, in the religious
sense of the word, a more mystical conception of the word
than that. The religious life is thus 'the high and mystic
communion that we have with Jesus Christ'.

It can be seen, then, that Calvin's 'theocentricity' never
led him to a piety which took him away from a living
relationship with Christ.

But whence then comes this hardness in the struggle
that we have described above and which has given
occasion to Calvin's numerous detractors to paint this
legendary caricature of an ambitious man who stopped at
nothing to gain his tyrannical ends?

In the certainty of being led by God there is an un-
shakable strength which gives the impression of ambition
to those who are outside the sphere of this activity. The
doggedness of a man who is led on by God is, for un-
believers, a proud desire to gain his own ends. Calvin
waged an incessant warfare in a town which had only
belonged to the Reformation for a few decades, and then
only in so far as a few outstanding individuals were concerned. The masses had not been won over and they

could ill bear the spiritual and moral direction that some of them had accepted. People who were desirous of living as they liked and for their own enjoyment, the older Genevan folk who complained of being led along by some French refugees in their own town, did all that they could to check the spiritual work of the preacher of the gospel. It was a struggle in a besieged town with many enemies within. Whilst the Reformation was being discussed at Geneva, it was being persecuted in France. The outcome of this struggle which he embarked upon so valiantly might have appeared doubtful. But Calvin kept in view the triumph of the cause of God. God must triumph. That was why the whole of his work has an element of the dramatic in it and is sometimes of a violent character.

Centuries have passed, however. The message of Calvinism has spread throughout the world. It has raised against every human pretension the demand of God the Lord. The Huguenots of the Cévennes, the Beghines in Holland, the Puritans in New England, the confessors of Hitler's Germany, have shown that, when the glory of God is threatened, men can resist oppression. The struggle continues. In this struggle Calvin will remain an indispensable guide and his word of command remains:

To God alone be the glory!

BIBLIOGRAPHICAL NOTES[1]

THE standard edition of Calvin's writings is a fifty-nine-volume set: *Johannis Calvini Opera quae supersunt omnia* (ed. H. W. Baum, E. Cunitz, E. Reuss, P. Lobstein and A. Erichson; Brunswick 1863–1900), referred to as *Op. Calv.* in the footnotes. They form volumes XXIX to LXXXVII of the *Corpus Reformatorum*. The final volume contains a full bibliography of Calvin studies up to 1900. Supplementing this, there is a complete bibliography of English books and articles on Calvin from 1900 to 1940 in the April, 1946, number of *The Evangelical Quarterly* (pp. 123 ff.), by T. H. L. Parker. The most recent bibliographical survey is in French, by W. Niesel: 'Ou en sont les publications calviniennes?' (*La Revue Réformée*, 1959, no. 2, pp. 1 ff.).

The most scholarly editing of any of Calvin's works is that done by P. Barth, W. Niesel and D. Schürer in *Opera Selecta Johannis Calvini* (Munich, 1926–1952). Vol. I of this set contains Calvin's writings from 1533 to 1541, Vol. II contains smaller works produced between 1542 and 1564, and Vols. III–V consist of a critical edition of the Latin *Institutes*, tracing its growth from the first version of 1536 through successive revisions to its final form (1559).

There is a comparable critical edition of the 1560 French text of the *Institutes* by J.-D. Benoit (Paris, 1957) and a modernized version of this text has been produced by J. Cadier and P. Marcel (Geneva, 1955–58).

Three English renderings of the *Institutes* have been

---

[1] These notes for English readers have been kindly contributed by J. I. Packer, M.A., D.Phil.

made, of which the first, by Thomas Norton (1561), was undoubtedly the best. The versions by Allen (1813) and Beveridge (1845) have often been reprinted (the latter is currently published by the Wm. B. Eerdmans Co. and by James Clarke [two vols., 1,300 pp.]) but they were both produced in an age when the translator's art was not well understood, and the flatness of Allen and the crabbed paraphrasing of Beveridge do not serve Calvin's lucid and lively Latin at all satisfactorily. The S.C.M. Library of Christian Classics is to include a new translation by J. T. McNeill; it will be better than Beveridge, no doubt, but it may well cost a good deal more. A fascinating background study that deserves mention here is B. B. Warfield's 'On the literary history of Calvin's "Institutes" ', in *Calvin and Calvinism* (New York, 1931).

Some of Calvin's occasional writings were brought out in English between 1844 and 1851 under the discouraging general title of *Tracts*; these have recently been reprinted as *Tracts and Treatises*, with a new introduction by T. F. Torrance (Eerdmans, Grand Rapids, 1958; Oliver and Boyd, Edinburgh, 1960). Other smaller works are contained in the Library of Christian Classics volume of Calvin's *Theological Treatises* (ed. J. K. S. Reid, S.C.M., 1954). Henry Cole published translations of *The Eternal Predestination of God* and *A Defence of the Secret Providence of God*, under the title of *Calvin's Calvinism* in 1855 and 1856, and these were later reprinted in one volume by the Sovereign Grace Union.

Calvin's catechetical writings, with their plainness of statement and practical religious purpose, are in some ways the best introduction to his thought. His *Instruction in Faith* (1537,) translated and edited by Paul T. Fuhrmann, was published by the Lutterworth Press in 1949; his *Catechism of the Church of Geneva* is in *Tracts and Treatises*,

II, 33 ff. and in *The School of Faith,* ed. T. F. Torrance, pp. 3 ff. (James Clarke, 1959).

Serviceable English renderings of all Calvin's commentaries were produced by the Calvin Translation Society of Edinburgh (forty vols., 1843–1855). Oliver and Boyd are now in process of publishing with Eerdmans new and more accurate versions of those on the New Testament. *John 1–10* and *1 Corinthians,* the two volumes which have so far appeared, are models of what translations of Calvin should be. Meanwhile Eerdmans in America also keep the older set of translations in print.

It is good to meet Calvin in his everyday work as a preacher and pastor. T. H. L. Parker has written a fine study of his preaching (*The Oracles of God,* Lutterworth Press, 1947) and translated his sermons on Isaiah liii (*Sermons on Isaiah's Prophecy of the Death and Passion of Christ,* James Clarke, 1956). For those who read French, J.-D. Benoit, *Calvin, Directeur d'Ames* (Strasbourg, 1946) provides an outstandingly attractive introduction to Calvin through his pastoral correspondence.

The first life of Calvin to be written, by his friend and successor at Geneva, Theodore Beza, will be found translated in the first volume of the *Tracts.* Good modern lives of Calvin have been produced by Williston Walker (1906) and R. N. Carew Hunt (1933). Two small introductory works of merit are T. H. L. Parker's *Portrait of Calvin* (S.C.M., 1955) and the older work of E. Stickelberger, *Calvin* (in German, Gotha, 1931; in English, published by James Clarke, 1959). Those who read French will find a vast store of historical matter in E. Doumergue's monumental *Jean Calvin, les Hommes et les Choses de son Temps* (seven vols., Lausanne and Paris, 1899–1927).

Calvin's letters are of absorbing interest for the light which they throw, not only on his work and influence, but on the man himself. About four thousand of them remain to us; these are collected in Vols. X to XX of the Brunswick edition. Some six hundred of them were put into English a century ago from the edition of J. Bonnet and published at Philadelphia in four volumes (the first two of which were also printed at Edinburgh, in 1855 and 1857). They are soon to be made available in Great Britain by the Banner of Truth Trust, and in America by Eerdmans. The latter edition will include letters hitherto untranslated into English.

It is better and safer to read Calvin than books purporting to expound Calvin; but some of the more helpful of these may be mentioned. Perhaps the most adequate general introductions to Calvin's theology are E. A. Dowey, *The Knowledge of God in Calvin's Theology* (Columbia University Press, New York, 1952); W. Niesel, *The Theology of Calvin* (in German, Munich, 1938, in English, Lutterworth Press, 1956); and, for those who read French, F. Wendel, *Calvin: Sources et Evolution de sa Pensée Religieuse* (Paris, 1950). *Calvinism*, by A. Dakin (Duckworth, 1940) is a slighter work. *The Teaching of Calvin*, by A. Mitchell Hunter (2nd edn. published by James Clarke, 1950) is admirable on all that it deals with, but does not carry the reader very deep into Calvin's mind.

Instructive studies on particular themes in Calvin have been produced by the following, among others: B. B. Warfield (articles on the knowledge of God, the nature of God, the Trinity and creation, in *Calvin and Calvinism* [New York, 1931]; all save the last named have reappeared in *Calvin and Augustine* [Presbyterian and Reformed Publishing Co., Philadelphia, 1956]); R. S. Wallace (*Calvin's Doctrine of the Word and Sacrament* [Eerdmans; Oliver and Boyd, 1953], *Calvin's Doctrine of the Christian Life* [Eerdmans; Oliver and Boyd, 1959]); Paul van Buren (*Christ in our*

Place: the substitutionary Character of Calvin's Doctrine of Reconciliation [Eerdmans; Oliver and Boyd, 1957]); T. F. Torrance (*Calvin's Doctrine of Man* [Eerdmans; Lutterworth Press, 1949]); H. Quistorp (*Calvin's Doctrine of the Last Things* [in German, Gütersloh, 1941; in English, Lutterworth Press, 1955]) and T. H. L. Parker (*The Doctrine of the Knowledge of God* [Oliver and Boyd, 1952; Eerdmans, rev. ed. 1959]). The student will find, however, that Calvin makes richer and more straightforward reading than any of his expositors.